Information Literacy: A Practitioner's Guide

CHANDOS
INFORMATION PROFESSIONAL SERIES

Series Editor: Ruth Rikowski
(email: rikowski@tiscali.co.uk)

Chandos' new series of books are aimed at the busy information professional. They have been specially commissioned to provide the reader with an authoritative view of current thinking. They are designed to provide easy-to-read and (most importantly) practical coverage of topics that are of interest to librarians and other information professionals. If you would like a full listing of current and forthcoming titles, please visit our web site **www.chandospublishing.com** or contact Hannah Grace-Williams on email info@chandospublishing.com or telephone number +44 (0) 1865 884447.

New authors: we are always pleased to receive ideas for new titles; if you would like to write a book for Chandos, please contact Dr Glyn Jones on email gjones@chandospublishing.com or telephone number +44 (0) 1865 884447.

Bulk orders: some organisations buy a number of copies of our books. If you are interested in doing this, we would be pleased to discuss a discount. Please contact Hannah Grace-Williams on email info@chandospublishing.com or telephone number +44 (0) 1865 884447.

Information Literacy: A Practitioner's Guide

SUSIE ANDRETTA

Chandos Publishing

Oxford · England · New Hampshire · USA

Chandos Publishing (Oxford) Limited
Chandos House
5 & 6 Steadys Lane
Stanton Harcourt
Oxford OX29 5RL
UK
Tel: +44 (0) 1865 884447 Fax: +44 (0) 1865 884448
Email: info@chandospublishing.com
www.chandospublishing.com

Chandos Publishing USA
3 Front Street, Suite 331
PO Box 338
Rollinsford, NH 03869
USA
Tel: 603 749 9171 Fax: 603 749 6155
Email: BizBks@aol.com

First published in Great Britain in 2005

ISBN:
1 84334 065 8 (paperback)
1 84334 066 6 (hardback)

© S. Andretta, 2005

Cover images courtesy of Bytec Solutions Ltd (*www.bytecweb.com*) and David Hibberd (*DAHibberd@aol.com*).

Printed in the UK and USA.

For Richard

Contents

Acknowledgements

I am indebted to Alan Bundy, University Librarian at the University of South Australia and editor of the Australian and New Zealand Institute for Information Literacy's framework; Hugh Thompson, Association of Colleges and Research Libraries Publications Manager; and Hilary Johnson, Chief Librarian at the University College Northampton and Chair of the Advisory Committee on Information Literacy, for permitting the reproduction of the three information literacy frameworks in this publication. My thanks go to Kathy Ennis, Senior Adviser at the Chartered Institute of Library and Information Professionals' Department of Knowledge & Information, for the provision of relevant material in the analysis of information literacy in the UK. I am particularly grateful to Alan Bundy for the invaluable resources provided on the Australian perspective of information literacy and for contributing the foreword for this book. Finally I would like to thank Terry Beck for the helpful comments on the manuscript and Adam Benjamin for editing the images used throughout the book.

List of figures and tables

Figures

Tables

List of abbreviations

ACRL	Association of Colleges and Research Libraries
AHRB	Arts & Humanities Research Board
AIR	Applied Information Research
ALA	American Library Association
ALIA	Australian Library and Information Association
ANZIIL	Australian and New Zealand Institute for Information Literacy
ASLIB	The Association for Information Management
CAUL	Council of Australian University Librarians
CHE	Commission on Higher Education
CILIP	Chartered Institute of Library and Information Professionals
CPD	continuing professional development
DfES	Department of Education and Skills
ECDL	European Computer Driving Licence
FE	further education
HE	higher education
HEA	Higher Education Academy
ICT	information and communication technologies
IIL	Institute of Information Literacy
IQ	institutional quotient
IT	information technology
LIC	Library and Information Commission
LIS	library and information science

LTSN-ICS	Learning & Teaching Support Network for Information and Computer Sciences (now renamed HEA-ICS [Higher Education Academy for Information and Computer Sciences])
MSU	Montana State University
OECD	Organisation for Economic Cooperation and Development
OU	Open University
SCIE	Social Care Institute for Excellence
SCONUL	Society of College, National and University Libraries
SWAP-ltsn	Social Policy and Social Work Learning & Teaching Support Network (now HEA SWAP)
UNESCO	United Nations Educational, Scientific and Cultural Organisation
VLE	virtual learning environment
WILL	World Initiative on Lifelong Learning

Foreword

Information can be transformational. Used well, it liberates and changes people, perceptions, society and improves lives. It also, in words attributed to Thomas Jefferson, 'is the currency of democracy'. If thinking is analysis of information, the key outcome of twenty-first-century education has to be people meeting the Socratic ideal of challenging lazy assumptions through their capacity to explore complex issues by generating webs of questions.

In 1920 H. G. Wells, in *The Outline of History*, asserted that 'Human history becomes more and more a race between education and catastrophe'.[1]

Yet education is of two kinds. As Illich (1976) and Freire (1974) concluded, it is never neutral. It domesticates or it liberates, the former occurring where knowledge is deposited into learners and where the relationship between educators and learner is that of subject to object. Education, in that race with catastrophe, must therefore surely seek not to domesticate, but to liberate.

That liberation mandates growing the global community of the informed and questioning as fast as possible. Whatever myriad issues challenge our world – environmental, health, political, democratic, economic, cultural or racial – responses to them require people who recognise their own need for good information, and who can identify, access, evaluate, synthesise and apply the required information. In other words, people who are information-literate.

That recognition of information *need* tends to be overlooked as the primary indicator of the information-literate person, as contrasted with a person merely possessing some information skills. Yet as the nineteenth-century British Prime Minister and novelist Benjamin Disraeli put it: 'To be conscious that you are ignorant is a great step to knowledge'.[2] Or as Sir Michael Caine, the British actor, has stated: 'I educated myself in the library, which means I found out for myself what I wanted to know. School taught me what I didn't know and what

I should find out when I left school. School should really teach you how ignorant you are and what you want to find out'.[3]

We tend to see ourselves in the twenty-first century as overwhelmed by change and information from all directions. However, in the 1860s commentators were lamenting the speed of change, travel and the stress created by overabundant information. A catalyst for the identification of information literacy as the functional literacy of the twenty-first century has thus been building for 150 years. There remains – in Britain in particular – a coyness about the term 'information literacy', although it comprises two common words, first linked by US educator Paul Zurkowski in 1974.[4] This was about the time that the educational icon of the twenty-first century, lifelong learning, also entered the language of formal and informal education. As Curran has pointed out, those two words, information and literacy, are understood by educated people. Information means interpreted data, news or facts. Literacy is conventionally the ability to read but is now widely associated with a capacity to understand or to interpret specific phenomena.

Combined, information and literacy are appropriate to describe the understandings and capacities essential in a post-industrial developed world where information, however it is provided and accessed, is the pervasive commodity, and where the requirements of society give importance to the concept. Information literacy was a long-standing need awaiting a descriptor, which it received only 30 years ago. Since then it has rapidly evolved into an umbrella concept, as a way of learning through engaging with information, and as a driver of pedagogical change for student-centred learning. It is developing as a field of research, scholarship and educational practice in response to recognition that within formal education, in the broadest sense of the words, it must be taught and not left to chance and osmosis. There is even slow recognition that it is the connecting issue for all three of the formal educational silos – primary, secondary and tertiary – about which much greater collaboration is required.

In 1758 Melchior von Grimm wrote: 'Every week new writings on education appear' and in 1762 he again remarked, 'the rage this year is to write on education'.[5] Something similar could be said about publication on information literacy since the 1990s. Most of this publication is to be found in conference proceedings or journals, but not enough of it is grounded in practice and research. A welcome contribution to the exploration of the mosaic of information literacy is therefore this book, on which its author and its publisher are to be congratulated.

In it, Susie Andretta provides a timely and valuable exploration and analysis of two models of information literacy, the one pursued in higher education in Britain, and the other in the USA, Australia and New Zealand.

Information Literacy: A Practitioner's Guide also highlights that information literacy is at a crossroads, needing to move beyond the generic skills development on which librarians have focused when faced with an absence of support from academic leaders and teachers for an integrated pedagogical approach to the subject.

Futurist Kim Long (1989) dismissed information literacy as yet another faddish educational buzzword. It clearly is not. As Professor Phil Candy, one of Australia's most respected educational researchers has observed

> ... information literacy is the *zeitgeist* of the times ... an idea whose time has at long last come. It is consonant with the reform agendas in government, in communications technology and in education ... with employers' demands for an adaptable and responsive workforce. It is increasingly multidisciplinary and must be included across the curriculum at whatever level of education or training ... and finally it is consistent with the notion of lifelong learning and the fact that the only constant is change. (Candy, 1996: 139).

In the conglomerated higher education systems of developed countries, educational change focused on the information realities and opportunities of the twenty-first century is required. Librarians are aware of that need for educational change from their long experience of interacting with information illiterate students. In this book, all educators, and particularly those responsible for strategies for educational change, are the practitioners. In their hands lies the development of information-literate and questioning people able to learn for life – but as importantly is the need to sustain open societies which, post September 11 2001, will surely be under increasing duress.

Dr Alan Bundy
University of South Australia

Notes

1. H.G. Wells quote accessible at: *http://www.quotationspage.com/quote/26977
   .html* (accessed 28 October 2004).
2. B. Disraeli quote accessible at: *http://www.quotationspage.com/quote/2061
   .html* (accessed 28 October 2004).
3. M. Caine quote accessible at: *http://www.embassy.org.nz/encycl/capedia.htm*
   (accessed 28 October 2004).
4. Zurkowski quote accessible at: *http://www.slais.ubc.ca/courses/libr500/
   03-04-wt2/www/M_Fowler/definitions.htm* (accessed 28 October 2004).
5. See Cipolla (1969).

About the author

Susie Andretta is a Senior Lecturer in Information Management in the Department of Applied Social Sciences, London Metropolitan University in the UK. Born in Italy, she has spent many years in Britain where she has completed degrees in the social sciences and cultural studies as well as becoming a professionally qualified teacher.

During her academic career she has conducted consultancy work for the British Council to enhance curriculum provision by the Institute of Library Studies at the University of Sierra Leone, has participated in a Tempus project funded by the European Union on curriculum development for the Department of Information and Communication at the University of Vilnius in Lithuania and has worked as a consultant for the Department for International Development (DfID – UK) in collaboration with the Ukrainian Academy of Public Administration (UAPA) and the World Bank to develop a distance learning programme of in-service training for practising civil servants.

Her current teaching responsibilities at the London Metropolitan University cover the implementation of information literacy education at all levels of provision. These include postgraduate courses on research design skills for the MA in Information Services Management, where information literacy is explored from a reflective information practitioner perspective, while at undergraduate degree level she has integrated information literacy programmes within disciplines such as law, social sciences and social work.

Her research interests complement her teaching practices by focusing on the impact of information literacy education at different levels of provision and in a range of disciplines. These projects, funded by the Higher Education Academy's subject centres for Social Policy and Social Work and Information and Computer Sciences, have led to the development of the web-based Information Literacy Gateway (*http://www.ilit.org*), which supports information literacy provision at London Metropolitan University. The author has contributed to a number of information literacy events including a seminar on the information literacy strategy in Finland organised by the Finnish Research Library Association and the Council for Finnish University Libraries and a workshop on the impact of information literacy organised by Yorkshire University Libraries in Leeds, UK. The author's publication profile also includes issues such as the need for visual information literacy within the library, the role of information literacy in the UK's key skills initiatives and the impact of information literacy integration within the British HE context.

The author can be contacted at the following address:

Susie Andretta
Senior Lecturer in Information Management
London Metropolitan University
62–66 Highbury Grove
London
N5 2AD

E-mail: *s.andretta@londonmet.ac.uk*
Website: *http://www.ilit.org*

Introduction

This book explores information literacy in the context of independent and lifelong learning, where the emphasis rests on the process of knowledge construction by the learner[1] and the facilitation of this practice by the information literacy educator. This role is necessarily broad, as it refers both to faculty staff from a range of subjects involved in the delivery of information literacy programmes and to information professionals, the majority from a library background, who are responsible for the provision of information literacy. Given the variety of information literacy educators, this book is directed at a wide readership. It is written from the perspective of a practitioner reflecting on concrete examples of information literacy provision set within a higher education (HE) institution.[2] The impact of information literacy practice is therefore assessed in terms of students' feedback and also in terms of the educator's own reflection in response to the students' input, in an attempt to explore issues of significance to information literacy educators operating within the HE environment. Relevant issues examined include the identification of the most appropriate information literacy skills to suit first-year undergraduate-level provision when dealing with predominantly mature students,[3] and the strategy of integration adopted to embed information literacy education within a professionally-oriented postgraduate programme.

There are three parts to this book. The first part is covered by Chapter 2 which sets the context by focusing on the independent-learning element of information literacy: the learning-how-to-learn approach, which is fundamental to achieve lifelong learning competences.[4] Profiles of approaches taken from the USA, Australia and the UK are used to illustrate the extent of the integration of information literacy initiatives within the three national learning agendas. Two different approaches emerge from this appraisal. The first model, found in the USA and Australia, shows that the challenges of lifelong learning are addressed through a clearly identified and coherent information literacy policy. This is reflected in the employment of predefined information literacy frameworks, devised by the US Association of Colleges and Research Libraries (ACRL)[5] and the Australian and New Zealand Institute for Information Literacy (ANZIIL)[6] respectively, that foster independent learning and develop effective information consumers. The promotion of a comprehensive integration strategy is also based on the active support for information literacy within the HE sector of these two countries. The second approach, adopted by the UK, although aiming to address the same lifelong learning challenges, is characterised by a technology-driven strategy in which information and communication technology (ICT) skills, and not information literacy competences, are prioritised in the national learning agenda. As a result, information literacy education in the UK features pockets of good practice, but lacks coherence at national level. From an information professional perspective, one of the main information literacy initiatives is illustrated by the information skills model devised by the Society of College, National and University Libraries (SCONUL) in 1999. This approach is used to structure information literacy provision in some British HE institutions,[7] but it is not widely promoted beyond academia, partly owing to the reluctance by the Chartered Institute of Library and Information Professionals (CILIP) to endorse its framework.

The second part of the book is covered by Chapter 3 which includes a comparison of the frameworks devised by ACRL, ANZIIL and SCONUL in order to provide a more comprehensive picture of the information literacy profile for each of the three countries examined.[8] Here the issue of integration is explored from the perspective of an HE institution, where strategies that foster high-order thinking and promote partnership between faculty, library and administrative staff are advocated.

The third and final part of the book focuses on information literacy practice, which is explored in Chapters 4–6. Chapter 4 introduces two case studies illustrating an information literacy provision that explores the dual perspective of the learner and that of professional practice. The learner's view is reflected by defining information literacy as an essential attribute of the successful independent learner. This principle was used to develop an information literacy module at the certificate level of a social sciences undergraduate scheme in 1999, and provides the focus for the first case study in Chapter 5. The description of information literacy as an essential competency for lifelong learning extends the boundaries of its transferability to reflect a more professionally-oriented perspective. This approach shaped information literacy provision at postgraduate level through the development of a research-based module, Applied Information Research (AIR), which addresses the independent and lifelong learning requirements of information practitioners. This module is explored in the second case study in Chapter 6. These two studies also exemplify methods of integrating an information literacy framework using generic and subject-specific models that suit a multidisciplinary context as well as different levels of provision, and therefore offer useful sources of comparison for information literacy educators involved in similar delivery. The generic approach is shown by provision at certificate level, where integration is achieved through subject-specific assessment tasks that also encourage the transferability of the information literacy skills. The subject-specific model is applied through the action research route (Moore, 2002) in order to achieve full integration of information literacy at programme level that enhances its professional relevance.

The most important theme that emerges from the exploration of information literacy presented in this book is the role that this concept can play in providing a framework for independent and lifelong learning to structure learning policies at national and HE institutional levels. Practice at London Metropolitan University, however, illustrates that the successful implementation of information literacy education depends on a substantial cultural shift within the academic environment, where learning is not focused exclusively on the acquisition of subject-specific knowledge, but on the students' ability to learn independently, supported by the tutor as a facilitator of this process through the active promotion of problem-solving and critical-thinking skills.

Notes

1. This is also referred to as the knowledge-spiral process (Bawden and Robinson, 2002), normally associated with postgraduate provision and with professional development.
2. London Metropolitan University, UK.
3. Also described as students who reach HE studies through non-traditional routes.
4. To paraphrase the Candy Report, lifelong learning refers to all types of learning, at any time and across the lifespan.
5. Association of Colleges and Research Libraries is a division of the American Library Association.

6. ANZIIL represents the information literacy approach adopted by both Australia and New Zealand; however, for the purpose of this book only the Australian perspective on information literacy is examined in detail.

7. For example, the SCONUL model was used to develop the Open University's MOSAIC and SAFARI information literacy programmes (Dillon et al., 2003).

8. This is the first time that these three information literacy frameworks have been displayed in a single publication to enable comparison. The full details of these frameworks are included as Appendices A, B and C.

Information literacy – setting the scene

How our country deals with the realities of the information age will have enormous impact on our democratic way of life and on our nation's ability to compete internationally. Within America's information society, there also exists the potential of addressing many long-standing social and economic inequities. To reap such benefits, people as individuals and as a nation must be information literate. (ALA, 1998)

From library instruction to information literacy

The aim of this chapter is to provide a picture of information literacy through the assessment of its origin, and the main initiatives that have led to its implementation as a framework for lifelong learning. Despite its wider significance within the educational environment, information literacy has evolved from library education practices, and therefore the debate presented here is based on the examination of the literature generated by the library and information science (LIS) disciplines. As the literature clearly illustrates, information literacy has developed to address the requirements generated by phenomena such as information overload caused by the rapid developments in digital technologies, by the needs of the information society for competent information consumers, and to meet the requirements of the knowledge economy for a responsive and informed workforce. This exploration of information literacy initiatives is based on the profiling of three English-speaking countries: the USA, Australia and the UK. The analysis presented here will assess the extent of these countries' overlap in their interpretation of information literacy, and will offer some comparison of the strategies they have adopted to incorporate information literacy programmes in their national learning agendas.

Definitions of library instruction

This section aims to identify the general characteristics of library instruction to set the historical context which defined the accepted strategies used prior to the introduction of information literacy education. Library instruction is often used interchangeably with bibliographic instruction, as they both involve: 'teaching the use of access tools such as catalogues of library holdings, abstracts, encyclopaedias, and other reference sources that aid library users searching for information' (Grafstein, 2002: 197). In the USA, during the early 1970s the Association of Colleges and Research Libraries (ACRL) described library instruction as the: 'provision of individual guidance in the use of materials and resources and in the interpretation of learning tools as well as formal instruction to groups' (Branch and Gilchrist, 1996: 447). By the early 1990s, this description had been redefined as: 'a programme to provide students bibliographic instruction through a variety of techniques enabling them to become information literate' (ibid.). The introduction of the concept of information literacy marks a fundamental shift in the pedagogy underpinning library instruction from being tutor-centred, in which instructions are imparted by a tutor at individual or group levels, to a student-centred, independent learning approach, as illustrated by the use of a variety of instructional techniques that address the needs of diverse users. This shift is also shown by changes in the mode of delivery, which has evolved from library tours and orientation lectures to fully integrated and accredited units that cover information-seeking practices. The latter is characterised by the provision of self-guided resources on general and subject-specific research activities. Such a flexible delivery also places the onus of learning on the student rather than on the librarian/tutor and fits in well with the student-centred, lifelong-learning strategies that characterise current higher education environments (Owusu-Ansah, 2004).

Mellon (1988) argued that the problem with traditional library instruction was its focus on discrete components of library activities that covered the use of the information tools, but did not explore the more complex tasks of information retrieval, based on critical thinking and evaluative skills. This limited scope therefore failed to encourage students to become independent library users. A similar perspective was presented by Oberman and Linton (1988) who at the time stated that bibliographic education concentrated on concrete skills-based processes of tools usage, and because of this it did not address the open-ended nature of research-based problem-solving tasks, characterised by reflective and critical thinking. As suggested by more recent literature, this view seems to ring as true today as it did then. For example, Lichtenstein (2000) claims that current practices of library instruction concentrate on activities that introduce students to the library environment, including its resources, services and the physical layout of its collection. The limitation of library education comes from the fact that it focuses the induction process on the use of a particular library, and, even when this covers digital information sources that are subject specific, it does not teach students how to be information literate. Grafstein (2002) concedes that distinctions between bibliographic instruction and information literacy are not always made explicit, although it is clear that the former covers resources that are physically bound to the library, whereas information literacy programmes address the need to access information increasingly accessible beyond the walls of the library and available in a variety of formats. She argues that during the 1990s, thanks to rapid developments in the digital information environment, library instruction within the American HE institutions has evolved from a sporadic service characterised by ad hoc delivery into fully contextualised information literacy practices. The importance of these programmes has been recognised by accrediting bodies that support the full integration of information literacy in the curriculum. For example, in 2000 the Information Literacy Competency Standards for HE were endorsed by the American Association for Higher Education, and in 1994 the Commission on Higher Education (CHE) published a set of standards describing information literacy as a main educational goal that: 'reaches far beyond the narrow concept of bibliographic instruction and touches both content and pedagogy' (CHE, 1994: vi). To achieve this goal, institutions are encouraged to provide access to the learning resources available: 'beyond the physical confines of the traditional library ... students, faculty and staff should have access to remote as well as on-site information resources'. (ibid.: v). These practices of information literacy involve not only the development of technical skills required to access digital information, but also include higher-level analytical and evaluative skills needed to engage effectively with the formulation of complex ideas. Lenox and Walker (1992: 4) envisage an information literacy approach that:

> ... allows us to express, to explore and to understand the flow of ideas among individuals and groups of people in a vastly changing technological environment ... the process, skills and habits of accessing and using ideas and information are undergoing revolutionary changes. Information Literacy refers ... to this set of complex, integrated, higher-level skills appropriate to our age.

Students' lack of information literacy skills

The need to expand the remit of library instruction is also generated by the students' lack of information and research skills. This problem was raised by Oberman (1991) in her study on American students, in which their inability to match subject relevance with appropriate sources of information and their unfamiliarity with the online environment led to an information excess that caused a considerable amount of anxiety. Over a decade later students are still faced with the problem of information anxiety, which Candy (2002) links to the impact of information explosion, or data smog, and which Bruce (2002), writing from an Australian perspective, associates with poor information literacy competences as learners cannot find the information they need and are forced to rely on others for its retrieval. Similar problems are shown by information literacy practice in other countries, thus making the lack of information literacy skills a global phenomenon. Hepworth's study on undergraduate students in Singapore,[1] for example, found that students were unable to formulate a search effectively as they 'tended to make a very literal interpretation of the question and started looking for material that mentioned those words listed in the question' (Hepworth, 1999). This study also shows that students experienced difficulties when attempting to implement a multiplicity of strategies requiring critical and lateral thinking, and when faced with a number of alternative outcomes. Similar findings were generated by a more recent study conducted in the UK by Andretta (2002) on a cohort of first-year undergraduate students attending the information literacy module at the University of North London.[2] Here the students' inability to cope with multiple answers to a given problem was compounded by a lack of critical thinking reflected by the difficulties of defining the focus of the topic of research and by their selection of inappropriate terminology and search strategies. In the USA, Stern's (2003) survey on the student population of a university in Michigan[3] has also produced a profile of Internet use, in which one-third of the respondents were unable to evaluate the source's reliability and quality. In addition, when tested on their ability to formulate a keyword search and to evaluate the credibility of a site by analysing its address, Stern found that:

> ... a large number of students, despite their confidence in their own information literacy for using the Internet for research, could benefit from systematic and cumulative formal instruction on Internet usage. (Stern, 2003: 117)

According to Oberman (1991) students must be equipped with critical thinking skills to counteract the problem of information overload and to be able to take advantage of the numerous choices offered by the electronic environment. This view is supported by Moore (2002), who states that the complexity of the current information environment requires skills that go beyond the ability to retrieve information from a limited range of sources. Here competences must include the ability to access information from complex information systems, to evaluate the content of the information in terms of authority and reliability and to apply the information found in a manner that fits the task.

Grafstein (2002), reflecting on the content of information literacy programmes, makes an important distinction between generic information skills and subject-specific competences of evaluating information. She identifies the skills required by the generic model as the formulation of one's information needs, the ability to break down the topic into keywords and the ability to combine these keywords into an effective search strategy. These competences are necessary to develop higher-level thinking skills and they therefore underpin research practices in any field. The evaluation of information, by contrast, varies according to the nature of the discipline explored and includes activities such as the assessment of timeliness, authority, bias, verifiability or use of evidence, and overall logical consistency. Grafstein points out that the implications generated by such a distinction are not fully acknowledged by the promoters of library education, but they play an important role in determining the content of information literacy provision.

Environmental factors in the shift to information literacy

The changes that brought about the need for information literacy were outlined by ALA's progress report in 1998:

> To respond effectively to an ever-changing environment, people need more than just a knowledge base, they also need techniques for exploring it, connecting to other knowledge bases, and making practical use of it. In other words the landscape upon which we used to stand has been transformed, and we are being forced to establish a new foundation called information literacy. Now knowledge – not minerals, or agricultural products or manufact- ured goods – is this country's [USA] most precious commodity, and people who are information literate – who know how to acquire knowledge and use it – are America's most valuable resources. (Owusu-Ansah, 2004: 4)

The recognition of rapid technological changes together with the proliferation of information sources that have initiated the shift from library instruction to information literacy are further documented by the ACRL Information Literacy Competency Standards for HE (ACRL, 2000):

> Because of escalating complexity of this [digital] environment, individuals are faced with diverse, abundant information choices – in their academic studies, in the workplace, and in their personal lives ... increasingly information comes to individuals in unfiltered formats, raising questions about its authenticity, validity, and reliability. In addition, information is available through multiple media, including graphical, aural, and textual, and these pose new challenges for individuals in evaluating and understanding it. (Lichtenstein, 2000: 25)

Lichtenstein (2000) attributes this threat of misinformation to the creative, and at the same time anarchic, nature of the Internet, where information is made available without being checked by rigorous editorial practices. These problems are addressed by ensuring that the user understands the process of information retrieval. This involves the ability to structure online searches through the correct manipulation of search vocabulary and strategies, as well as the assessment of the search results and the selection of relevant information that satisfies the initial enquiry. A similar view is promoted by SCONUL's (1999) paper on information skills, which specifically identifies students' over-reliance on the Internet as the main reason for the development of information literacy, and argues that the lack of credibility and reliability of Internet sources requires the development of critical analytical skills on the part of the user. The need for such a critical-thinking approach has shifted the emphasis in library instruction from the lower cognitive objectives of knowledge and comprehension, i.e. without the transferable-skills element, to the higher cognitive objectives of analysis, synthesis and evaluation underpinning the information literacy perspective. Oberman advocates the active-learning method to encourage the development of critical thinking through self-discovery and learning-by-doing strategies:

> Providing students with the cognitive tools to make informed decisions must become a keystone of library instruction. [Otherwise] students unable to cope with the overwhelming number of choices ... will be further disenfranchised from the information structure. (Oberman, 1991: 200)

This approach, Oberman concludes, gives the additional benefits of high retention of the information found and encourages the transferability of the skills developed during this investigative process to tackle new problems.

Bawden (2001) argues that the debate on bibliographic instruction and information literacy has generated much literature but does not offer any widely shared conclusions. However, Lenox and Walker draw one main distinction from this discussion by associating bibliographic instruction with situation- and task-specific conditions, while the link between information literacy and lifelong learning gives this concept a wide-ranging appeal because its transferability goes beyond the confines of library-based research and reflects:

> a conceptual framework for the development of educational models and new curricular concepts in systematically addressing information skill development in a diverse society [teaching information literacy involves] a curriculum and a pedagogy designed to help [the students] use their knowledge in deciding, acting and behaving in this world. (Lenox and Walker, 1992: 5)

Information literacy: a multifaceted concept

The surge of interest in information literacy is shown by Bawden's (2001) review of the literature, which illustrates that computer and library literacies have featured consistently throughout the 20-year period examined, whereas information literacy, which maintained a low profile in the 1980s, became the focus of rapidly increasing attention during the 1990s. Rader (2002b) confirms this steady rise of interest in the literature by establishing that over 5,000 articles have been produced on the subject since 1973, and that over 300 of these papers were published in 2002 alone compared with 28 publications reviewed in 1978. Although the concept of information literacy was first introduced by Paul Zurkowski as far back as 1974 (Bruce, 1997: 5), currently there is no single definition of this concept, and the term is often used interchangeably with computer literacy and bibliographic instruction (Kirk, 2002). However, according to Mutch (1997) the use of the term information literacy, generated by both computing and library science literature, is found wanting because it does not fully address the skills associated with the process of knowledge creation. In his view, information literacy must be placed above computer literacy because, whereas the latter focuses on the ability to use a computer, the former is strongly linked to lifelong learning. This point is fully supported by ACRL in its publication on Information Literacy Competency Standards, which states that 'information literacy initiates, sustains, and extends lifelong learning through abilities which may use technology but are ultimately independent of them' (ACRL, 2000: 5).

Candy recognises the difficulties when comparing information literacy to ICT literacy in an effort to identify distinguishing features between these two concepts. He argues that from the perspective of skills requirements, those needed to access and retrieve information are completely different from the competence required in assessing the information. However, a degree of overlap between these two processes occurs because 'information in the digital environment is at least partly an artefact of the technology itself' (Candy, 2002: 7). By this he means that the unpredictable nature of web pages, for example, is intrinsically linked to the knowledge of web technology and has an impact on the skills needed to assess the reliability of such a source. He concludes that 'the evaluation of information in the digital environment is a challenging matter, and one that cannot readily be divorced from the technological competence of the inquirer' (ibid.: 8). Kirk (2002), by contrast, asserts that the nature of information literacy is multifaceted and that this concept can only be defined by placing other forms of literacies, including tool literacy, resource literacy, social-structural literacy, research and publishing literacies, as its subcategories.

Moore acknowledges that the interpretation of information literacy varies considerably, from the attainment of computer literacy to the development of library skills, and it also includes the control of information and the establishment of knowledge construction. To counteract this multitude of perspectives, she proposes a broader description and defines information literacy as the 'mastery of the processes of becoming informed' (Moore, 2002: 2). This process stresses the importance of information literacy as a pedagogical tool, in which a number of practices converge, including resource-based learning, constructivist and meta-cognitive theories as well as the development of thinking skills through modelling and scaffolding. It also draws on critical thinking and problem solving, as well as the implementation of information practices and systems within the academic environment and beyond. Similarly, Bruce argues that information literacy education supports deep learning based on the learner-centred approach, which gives the opportunity 'to transform dependent learners into independent, self-directed, lifelong learners' (Bruce, 2002: 5).

Richard Paul, in an insightful paper on critical thinking, explains that this approach entails developing an independent, lifelong learning attitude through the distinction of this type of high-order thinking from lower-order rote learning,[4] and stresses that:

> Higher-order learning multiplies comprehension and insight; lower-order rote memorisation multiplies misunderstanding and prejudice. Higher-order learning stimulates and empowers, whereas lower-order learning discourages and limits the learner. Although very little instruction is deliberately aimed at lower-order learning, that type of learning most often emerges [and] few students understand what it means to think analytically through the content of a subject; few use critical thinking as a tool for acquiring knowledge [and as a result students] end their schooling with a jumble of fragmentary opinions, rigidly understood procedures, and undisciplined beliefs. They have gained little knowledge or insight. They are at best trained, not educated, not critical thinkers or persons. As a result, their adaptability, their capacity to learn on the job and in their personal and civic lives, is severely limited.

> Their ability to mature intellectually and morally, and their capacity and motivation to learn, are stunted. (Paul, 1992: 4)

Paul elaborates on the process required to become a critical thinker by promoting the use of investigation to gain long-lasting knowledge. This investigative process includes: the evaluation of an initial problem or question; the assessment and understanding of the purpose or goal of the problem set; consideration of the frame of reference or points of view underpinning the investigation; review of the assumptions made when engaging with the question; the evaluation of core concepts and ideas involved and of the principles or theories underpinning these; the critical assessment of evidence used to support the interpretations and claims arrived at by this process; and finally the analysis of any inferences derived from this thought-process and any implications generated by them.

Bawden and Robinson (2002) quote a similar approach, illustrated by the work of Gibson and Meade, to describe critical thinking within the context of information literacy. Like Paul, they refer to this term as 'a disciplined process' (Bawden and Robinson, 2002: 300), and identify comparable stages required to engage with critical thinking in the course of an investigation, although the emphasis here is focused on the knowledge-spiral element of this process of research. The stages identified include:

> ... asking informed questions; posing problems in various ways before attempting to solve them; examining assumptions; solving ill-structured, messy, 'real-world' problems; evaluating sources of information; assessing the quality of one's own thinking and problem solving. (Bawden and Robinson, 2002: 300)

In practice the capacity for critical thinking is normally associated with the advanced level of the learning spectrum and with research methods, modules or dissertation work, where the emphasis is on the development of independent research skills.[5]

Information literacy and the 'learning how to learn' approach

The broadest definition commonly used as a starting point for information literacy education was provided by ALA in 1989. Here the competences of information practices reflect the stages involved in critical thinking identified above. This process encourages independent learning and, by implication, it promotes lifelong learning.

> To be information literate, a person must be able to recognize when information is needed and have the ability to locate, evaluate, and use effectively the needed information. Producing such a citizenry will require that schools and colleges appreciate and integrate the concept of information literacy into their learning programs and that they play a leadership role in equipping individuals and institutions to take advantage of the opportunities inherent within the information society. Ultimately, information literate people are those who *have learned how to learn*. They know how to learn because they know how knowledge is organized, how to find information, and how to use information in such a way that others can learn from them. They are people prepared for lifelong learning, because they can always find the information needed for any task or decision at hand. (ALA, 1989)

According to Webber and Johnston (2000) the comparison of definitions on information literacy reveals a common coverage of the stages of information need recognition, search formulation, source selection and interrogation, information evaluation, information synthesis and use. This is reflected in the information literacy approach promoted by Doyle (1992). In this model an information-literate person is able to: recognise the need for information; appreciate the importance of accurate and complete information to make intelligent decisions; identify potential sources of information; develop appropriate search strategies to access sources of information irrespective of the technology; evaluate information and organise this for practical purposes, and, lastly, integrate information into an existing body of knowledge. A similar approach is illustrated by the work of Eisenberg and Berkowitz (1990), which is defined by Bruce (2002) as systematic information behaviour that involves: task definition; development of information seeking strategies; locating and accessing the information; using information; synthesising and evaluating information. The main distinction between these two perspectives is that Doyle fully contextualises the information literacy process in critical-thinking and problem-solving settings.

Hepworth (2000) offers a detailed diagrammatic representation of the process involved in becoming information literate, which identifies four main areas of learning that, in his view, need to be mastered. This model supports the description of information literacy as a multifaceted term encompassing all other forms of literacies and providing a useful framework that can be applied to embed information literacy in the curriculum. Although Hepworth (2000) warns that some aspects of these areas will vary, for example the intellectual norms will change in line with the epistemological characteristics of a given discipline, the main areas of learning apply to all disciplines and are described as follows (Figure 2.1):[6]

- learning how to use information tools, including interaction with software and navigation of information systems (electronic and printed);

- learning the intellectual processes dealing with information management and knowledge creation, such as identification of information needs, key concepts, searching and retrieval strategies, organisation of resources gathered and reflection skills;

- learning how to communicate – involves skills associated with exchange and sharing of information, such as team work, negotiating, collaborative work as well as appropriate communication styles;

- learning the intellectual norms of the subject explored, including established theoretical framework and methodologies, as well as the ethical and legal issues related to that domain.

Figure 2.1   Key areas of learning (Hepworth, 2000: 24).

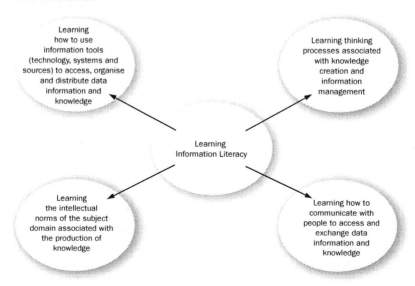

Models of information literacy

Bruce identifies three main approaches characterising information literacy: the behaviourist, the constructivist and the relational models. To describe the behaviourist approach, Bruce quotes Rowntree's interpretation of this model as: 'a psychological theory based on the analysis of observable behaviour' (Bruce, 1997: 36). Here information literacy is defined in terms of attributes and skills that can be learned and objectively measured.[7] Bruce criticises the behaviourist approach because of its emphasis on measuring discrete competences, which, in her view, is:

> Fundamentally at odds with the very idea of information literacy which suggests that knowledge and skills are quickly outdated, and that information literacy involves being able to learn and relearn in the face of constant change. (Bruce, 1997: 39)[8]

Introduced as an alternative to the behaviourist perspective, the constructivist approach is characterised by 'mental models, and associated with the learning-how-to-learn perspectives' where the individual is seen as constructing his/her own representation of what is being learned, and where the emphasis is on the development of critical thinking and problem-solving competences. Although this perspective is used to shape information literacy provision, Bruce argues that 'at present its influence on thinking about information literacy continues to grow, but has not displaced the skills based approaches that dominate'[9] (Bruce, 1997: 37). In addition to the principles of independent learning and critical thinking commonly found in constructivist practices, the relational model promotes the development of personal values that encourage the critical use of information, the acquisition of sound knowledge of the information environments and a personal information style that facilitates the learner's interaction with the world at large. The fundamental shift is in the way Bruce focuses on people's conceptions of information literacy, rather than on the assessment of measurable attributes and skills:

> Describing information literacy in terms of the varying ways in which it is experienced by people, that is their conceptions, is the alternative which I propose. Studying information literacy from the viewpoint of the people ... is the first step towards a relational view of information literacy. (Bruce, 1997: 39)

By adopting the perspective of the user, this model promotes an experiential approach that depicts the interaction between the user and his/her surrounding, stresses the relationship between the user and information and promotes the view of users rather than that of experts.[10] The relational model frames information literacy into seven different ways of experiencing information use through the learner's active and reflective engagement with the relevant information practices. This approach therefore focuses on the user's interpretation, or conception, of the various stages of information literacy. These are:

- *Information technology (IT) conception*, which associates information literacy with the use of IT to gather and communicate information.

- *Information sources conception*, in which information literacy is perceived as the knowledge of sources and the ability to access these directly, or indirectly via an intermediary.

- *Information processing conception.* Information literacy here is seen as 'executing a process' (Bruce, 1997: 128), in which a new situation is tackled through the use of an appropriate strategy to find and use information. The nature of the process varies according to the participant who is engaging in this process.

- *Information control conception.* Information literacy here is associated with the effective control and manipulation of information through the use of mechanical devices, memory or IT.

- *Knowledge construction conception*, in which information literacy is perceived as 'building a personal knowledge base in a new area of interest' (Bruce, 1997: 137). Bruce stresses that this differs from the storage of information, because it involves the application of critical analysis of the information read.

- *Knowledge extension conception*, which envisages the application of knowledge and personal perspectives that lead to new insights.

- *Wisdom conception*, which is associated with the wise and ethical use of information considered in a wider historical or cultural context, such as historical or cultural perspectives. In addition, the information here undergoes 'a process of reflection which is part of the experience of effective information use' (Bruce, 1997: 148).

The stigma of literacy?

The literature describes information literacy as a set of skills that go beyond retrieving and communicating information. Arp (1990) argues that in practice this concept is embedded in the general literacy debate, in which literacy is seen as a competence in communication skills that enable individuals to function within the social environment. It follows that the idea of literacy within an information society is valued for its functionality, i.e. the ability to use adequate information to address any situation at personal and professional levels. The term functional literacy was originally coined by the Organisation for Economic Cooperation and Development (OECD) in 1996 to describe the social purpose of the concept of literacy: 'using printed and written information to function in society in order to achieve one's goals, and to develop one's knowledge and potential'.[11] This definition is contrasted with the stark reality of functional illiteracy. For example, the study by Shapiro and Hughes (1996) showed that in the USA 40–50 per cent of the population fell into this category, and in the UK a similar study on literacy by the OECD in 2000 found that 22 per cent of the population in England and Wales were functionally illiterate.[12]

Moore (2002) confirms the claims that the concept of literacy and its educational value have acquired a social dimension by quoting the example of the Pisa 2000 study (OECD, 2002), which explores literacy within the context of reading, mathematics and science, and promotes the view that a threshold level of literacy within these contexts is required for an active participation in society. The implication for information literacy, Moore argues, is that we are dealing with more than just the ability to read and write. Rather, literacy in this context is perceived in its highest sense of interpretation and reflection. Despite this view, some information practitioners are reluctant to use the term 'literacy' because of the perceived association with the issue of illiteracy and 'the continuing implication that librarians are dealing with clients on a basic or even remedial level' (Snavely and Cooper, 1997: 10). In the UK, for example, the model promoted by SCONUL comes under the banner of information skills. Hilary Johnson, chair of the taskforce responsible for the development of this model, explains the concern over the term 'information literacy' and the rationale behind the adoption of 'skills' as a compromise:

> The question of terminology featured early on in our work ... We
> have continued to use the term 'information skills' ... rather than

formulations such as information literacy or information handling. The use of the word skills in certain sections of the UK HE scene is problematic, and we certainly feel that skills is too limiting a concept, because we feel real information literacy encompasses a range of cognitive as well as motor skills. However, literacy in some applications has a threshold meaning which we are also anxious to avoid. (Johnson, 2003: 48)

A more appropriate definition of higher literacy is used in this book, which 'entails the ability to make inferences from material, formulate questions and develop ideas' (Lichtenstein, 2000: 23). This description, therefore, elevates information literacy to a method of enquiry that is suitable for the HE environment, and one that operates at the knowledge-creation end of the learning spectrum. Bawden confirms this perspective by calling for a broad type of literacy, one that:

Must subsume all the skill-based literacies, but cannot be restricted to them, nor can it be restricted to any particular technology or set of technologies. Understanding, meaning and context must be central to it. (Bawden, 2001: 25)

A final distinction is made by ACRL between the terms *fluency* and *literacy* and their appropriate use within the information literacy debate. The former is associated with understanding the underlying concepts of technology and the application of technology for problem-solving practices. The latter, by contrast, when used in conjunction with information, 'provides an intellectual framework for under-standing, finding, evaluating, and using information activities' (ACRL, 2000: 2).

Information literacy and lifelong learning

Candy quotes the United Nations Educational, Scientific and Cultural Organisation (UNESCO)'s definition of lifelong learning which, as early as 1972, envisaged this process as 'the master concept for educational policies in the years to come for both developed and developing countries' (Candy, 2002: 2). A further description of lifelong learning, devised by the World Initiative on Lifelong Learning (WILL) in 1994, extends its range beyond the confines of formal education to all those involved in either the production or the consumption of information, and who operate at individual, community, national and international levels.

> A continuously supportive process which stimulates and empowers individuals to acquire all the knowledge, values, skills and understanding they will require throughout their lifetimes and to apply them with confidence, creativity and enjoyment in all roles, circumstances and environments. (ibid.)

Furthermore, in 1996 the OECD published a report entitled *The Knowledge-Based Economy* that strengthened the case for lifelong learning by stressing the importance of the ability to learn to fulfil increasing demands for highly-skilled workers.

> The knowledge-based economy is characterised by the need for continuous learning of both codified information and the competencies to use this information. As access to information becomes easier and less expensive, the skills and competencies relating to the selection and efficient use of information become more crucial ... Capabilities for selecting relevant information, recognising patterns in information, interpreting and decoding information as well as learning new and forgetting old skills are in increasing demand. (O'Sullivan, 2002: 8)

The above statements stress that the capacity for lifelong learning skills cannot be perceived as the domain of any specific discipline, but must be associated with general information seeking practices underlying the lifelong learning initiative. Moreover, Hepworth (1999), by describing a lifelong learner as someone who can educate him/herself, creates a strong association between this process and the learning-how-to-learn approach that underpins information literacy. In fact, according to Bruce (1999), the acknowledgment of lifelong learning as an educational goal was one of the main driving forces behind the development of information literacy as a global phenomenon.

The learning-how-to-learn perspective, originally proposed by ALA, involves the ability to locate, manage, critically evaluate and use information for problem solving, research, decision-making and continuous professional development. This is seen as a vital component for lifelong learning because it enables students to develop a framework for independent learning and transferable skills that can be applied to new situations and problems (Orr et al., 2001). Mutch (1997) also

Figure 2.2 Relationship between information literacy and lifelong learning (Bundy, 2004: 5).

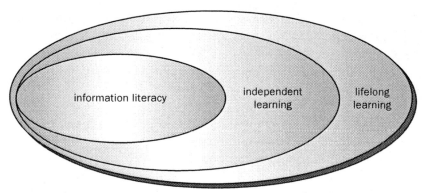

supports this view by stating that how we define and interpret information extends beyond the concern for the activities of storage and retrieval associated with knowledge transmission. By this he means that the process of interpretation consists of the formulation of questions in the pursuit of knowledge creation, the identification of the best way of accessing and storing data, and the acknowledgment of factors, operating at both individual and social levels, that influence the use of the data. This process provides the reflective element that links information literacy to lifelong learning and should inform national information policies as well as be embedded in the curricula of HE institutions and professional-development practices across all sectors.

In line with ALA's perspective, ANZIIL associates this concept with 'knowing how to learn' (Bundy, 2004: 5), and illustrates graphically how it operates as a subcategory of independent learning which, in turn, is a subset of lifelong learning (Figure 2.2).

ANZIIL's definition of lifelong learning is taken from the Candy Report (Candy et al., 1994) and covers: 'all formal, non-formal and informal learning – whether intentional or unanticipated – which occurs at any time across the lifespan' (Bundy, 2004: 4). The lifelong learner's profile promoted by the report is included in the standards to illustrate the high degree of overlap between this and information literacy. The profile presents the following features:[13]

- knowledge of major current resources available in at least one field of study;
- ability to frame researchable questions in at least one field of study;

- ability to locate, evaluate, manage and use information in a range of contexts;
- ability to retrieve information using a variety of media;
- ability to decode information in a variety of forms: written, statistical, graphs, charts, diagrams and tables;
- critical evaluation of information.

ANZIIL also argues that the self-directed and independent-learning approaches promoted by information literacy education are reflected in the adoption of a constructivist pedagogy which introduces learners to problem-based and resource-based learning through the experiential learning mode. The learning process in the constructivist environment is developed through question formulation and the framing of problems that emphasise, explicitly and implicitly, the effective use of information. A similar view is promoted by ACRL's information literacy standards underpinned by the view of the Boyer Commission, which supports the need to embed the lifelong learning perspective within a student-centred learning environment consisting of: '[the] framing of a significant question or set of questions, the research or creative exploration to find answers, and the communication skills to convey the results' (ACRL, 2000: 5).

The expansion of information literacy beyond an educational setting is supported by SCONUL's paper on information skills through the promotion of information literacy as an essential commodity for survival in a lifelong learning context. SCONUL calls on the educational sector to focus on the fostering of critical information consumers who are equipped with appropriate transferable skills required to cope with rapid technological and economic changes. This is also a central theme in the Candy report, in which becoming information literate is seen as a lifelong pursuit that should be promoted beyond the context of formal education to address the needs of the society as a whole. The report concludes that despite national developments towards the achievement of information economies and learning societies, in practice:

> Few, if any, national governments have committed to major educational or social initiatives that would see widespread adoption of information literacy training or assessment for their populations. Most initiatives tend to be piecemeal, in general aimed at limited sections of the population, such as school children, university students, library and information specialists, or those already within or wishing to enter the workforce. (Candy, 2002: 12)

Information literacy and the National Learning Agenda

Ford (1995) warns that the impact of the information society transcends political, economic and social boundaries, and that therefore national reforms must address the rapidly changing nature of information and IT, and must integrate information literacy in the educational experience to equip individuals with skills needed to deal with these challenges.

Bundy (1999) expands on this by claiming that the increased availability of information tools and rapid developments in ICT have enhanced physical access to information, but have not improved intellectual access, and that this has created a problem of information overload. He provides a detailed outline of the impact of this phenomenon:

> We are awash with information. The total of all printed information doubles every five years. More information has been generated in the last three decades than in all the previous 5000 put together. We are in the midst of an information explosion ... the casualties are mounting up [causing] a new ailment – information fatigue syndrome. (Bundy, 1999: 236–7)

Bundy comments further that the problem is particularly acute in relation to the Internet, where the development of a superhighway of information has not been paralleled by appropriate training of the drivers/users. He concludes that the introduction of information literacy is seen as fundamental in response to these challenges as it addresses the need of the global knowledge economy for an informed workforce. The strong link between information literacy and the global economy has often led researchers to explore information literacy provision from a global international perspective (Bruce, 1999; Bruce and Candy, 2000; Moore, 2002; Rader, 2003; Virkus 2003, among many others). The selection of the USA, UK and Australia in the following sections parallels the work by Stephen Town, who compares their respective information literacy policies on the basis that in these English-speaking countries 'information literacy appears to be a commonly understood concept' (Town, 2003: 86). Despite an overlap in their perspectives, the USA and Australia prefer to use the term information literacy, whereas in the UK the description of information skills is more commonly found (The Big Blue Project, 2001b[14]). Town also claims that the association between information literacy and the information society, where the former is needed to ensure that individuals function effectively in the latter, necessarily requires governments to include information literacy in national policies related to the information age and to the phenomenon of the global knowledge economy. He identifies three main drives underpinning the development of the information society: (1) the need at national level to be an effective competitor within the global knowledge economy; following from this, he identifies (2) the need to train the population to operate within this global economic environment, which leads to the development of a national learning agenda; lastly he explores (3) the need for information management skills at both individual and corporate levels to deal with the information overload caused by developments in digital media and communications technologies. This view is supported by Bundy (2001), who argues that:

> Information literacy is consonant with reform agendas in government, in communication technology and in education [as well as] with employers' demands for an adaptable and responsive workforce.

Examination of the national initiatives promoting information literacy presented here is also inspired by the work of Booth and Fabian, who advocate a campus-wide information literacy provision that reflects the 'learning goals articulated in national, institutional, departmental accreditation and curricular guidelines' (Booth and Fabian, 2002: 127). Their perspective is useful in creating a framework that enables the identification of information literacy standards and the assessment of how the educational targets underpinning these operate at national level.

Candy, however, warns that any examination of information literacy policies can only cover major initiatives, considering that:

> In a dynamic and fast-changing field such as this, it is difficult to be exhaustive at the national level, and even more impossible to identify useful projects and publications that are generated at the level of states, provinces or prefectures. (Candy, 2002: 13)

The following sections therefore provide a necessarily broad overview of the information literacy policies promoted by the USA, Australia and the UK. However, even through such a general analysis evidence shows that there is some degree of overlap between the HE conditions found in

Australia and those experienced by the UK, such as the 'disappearance of the binary divide between universities and degree-awarding colleges of advanced education in the late 1980s' (Bundy, 2001). Despite this similarity, The Big Blue Project (2001a) stresses that Australia has achieved a more comprehensive integration of information literacy within the HE sector than the UK. In Australia information literacy is promoted as the foundation of independent and lifelong learning, whereas in the UK the government's e-learning strategy defines information literacy as a necessary e-oriented skill, although it is the area of ICT that is specifically singled out as 'a priority for the new Skills Strategy'[15] (DfES, 2003). The comparison between the countries' profiles presented here shows that both the USA and Australia have implemented far more advanced information literacy policies, mainly owing to the active approaches adopted by their respective library and information professional associations and thanks to government strategies that make clear distinctions between information literacy competences and ICT fluency.

National perspectives on information literacy in the USA

The information literacy agenda in the USA was set as early as 1974 by a report produced by the Information Industry Association, although this perspective focused mainly on the impact of technology on information use and limited its contextualisation to the work environment. This initial interpretation of information literacy was later widened beyond the acquisition of computer skills, as illustrated by the Boyer Commission's report[16] on undergraduate education published in 1995, which claimed that graduates lacked the basic skills required to function in a professional world and illustrated students' unfamiliarity with the basics of research. The report also argued that to achieve an appropriate level of academic competence students must become intelligent information consumers who see information as 'an essential commodity for survival' (Doherty et al., 1999). The commission has provided a clear profile of information-literate students within the American HE sector:

> All graduates of baccalaureate programs must be able to recognise when they need information, what kind of information they need, and where to look for it to complete a task successfully.

They must also be able to do this effectively regardless of the information's format, source, or location. They must understand how information is structured and organised and how the structure, organisation, availability, and retrievability of information are influenced by the structure and organisation of the dominant society. (Doherty et al., 1999)[17]

At the time, the report challenged universities to shift provision from the traditional instructional model to an inquiry-based learning approach characterised by students' active engagement with the research process. This perspective is fully aligned with the definition of information literacy competences presented by ALA (1989), promoting the view that 'what is called for is not a new information studies curriculum, but, rather, a restructuring of the learning process' (Snavely and Cooper, 1997: 9). To implement a national information literacy policy the Information Literacy Competency Standards for Higher Education were devised by ACRL and formally approved by its Board of Directors in January 2000. These standards were later endorsed by the American Association for Higher Education and US accreditation bodies, thus ensuring a comprehensive and coherent execution of an information literacy strategy within this sector.[18] In addition, to prepare for this new information literacy education the Institute of Information Literacy (IIL)[19] was set up by ACRL in 1998 with the aim of providing intensive information literacy training programmes for librarians and information professionals in order to support actively the full integration of information literacy within all the educational contexts (Rader, 2002a). Booth and Fabian also present the legislation, GOALS 2000: Educate America Act, as a positive step towards the implementation of information literacy on a national scale. This is because the legislation reflects the need to develop 'national standards for student achievement, citizenship, adult literacy, and lifelong learning' (Booth and Fabian, 2002: 131), and these areas, they argue, rely on complex information skills such as critical thinking, evaluation and problem solving, which all come under the banner of information literacy.

ALA was also instrumental in the development of the National Forum on Information Literacy[20] in 1990, which is described by Oberman as 'a coalition of education associations outside of librarianship that focuses national attention on the importance of information literacy to individuals, the economy, and an informed citizenry'.[21] One of its primary roles is to promote debate on this at national and international levels, and in September 2003 the National Forum on Information Literacy co-sponsored an international conference in collaboration with UNESCO and the National Commission on Libraries and Information Science (NCLIS).[22] This event aimed to provide an opportunity for discussion on information literacy strategies in the following five environments: economic development, education, human services, library and information science, and policymaking.[23]

The conference has produced a final report entitled *The Prague Declaration: Towards an Information Literate Society*, which is based on the following five information literacy principles:[24]

- The creation of an information society is key to social, cultural and economic development of nations and communities, institutions and individuals in the twenty-first century and beyond.

- Information literacy encompasses knowledge of one's information concerns and needs, and the ability to identify, locate, evaluate, organise and to create, use and communicate effectively information to address issues or problems at hand; it is a prerequisite for participating effectively in the information society, and is part of the basic human right of lifelong learning.

- Information literacy, in conjunction with access to essential information and effective use of information and communication technologies, plays a leading role in reducing the inequities within and among countries and peoples, and in promoting tolerance and mutual understanding through information use in multicultural and multilingual contexts.

- Governments should develop strong interdisciplinary programmes to promote information literacy nationwide as a necessary step in closing the digital divide through the creation of an information literate citizenry, an effective civil society and a competitive workforce.

- Information literacy is a concern to all sectors of society and should be tailored by each to its specific needs and context.

- Information literacy should be an integral part of education for all, which can contribute critically to the achievement of the United Nations Millennium Development Goals, and respect for the Universal Declaration of Human Rights.

These principles offer a blueprint of information literacy that could influence not only educational but also economic and social developments within a global perspective. In addition, the Prague conference has taken the information literacy debate to an unprecedented level of international scrutiny by proposing an International Congress on Information Literacy in 2005 to review progress on the implementation of an information literacy policy by individual countries and through the proposal to promote information literacy as part of the United Nations Literacy Decade (2003–2012) initiative.

National perspectives on information literacy in Australia

Bundy (1999) describes a number of changes experienced by the Australian HE sector in the 1990s that have been instrumental in the introduction of an information literacy strategy. These include a rapid increase in the number of students entering HE; disappearance of the different status between universities and colleges, as well as the introduction of mergers that resulted in large universities;[25] greater reliance on non-governmental funding; a large number of overseas students; and the introduction of student-centred lifelong learning strategies. The initial step towards the official recognition of information literacy was made by the *Review of Library Provision in Higher Education Institutions*[26] published in 1990. Included in its terms of reference were: 'the role of higher education libraries in preparing those training for the professions in information literacy' (The Big Blue Project, 2001a).

The importance of information literacy was further acknowledged by a number of government publications listed in the first edition of the *Information Literacy Standards*, published by the Council of Australian University Librarians (CAUL, 2001). Among the examples quoted by CAUL, is the 1991 report of the House of Representatives Committee for Long-term Strategies on Australia as an information society. This report openly promoted 'the need to introduce information literacy programs at all levels of education to develop information handling skills in students' (CAUL, 2001: 13). Following from this, in 1992, the Meyer Committee produced a report on *Employment Related Key Competencies for Post Compulsory Education and Training*,[27] which defined the main inform-ation literacy practices such as collecting, analysing and organising ideas and information as essential prerequisites for the development of an effective workforce. A further interpretation was added in 1994 by the report *Developing Lifelong Learners Through Undergraduate Education* produced by Candy, Crebert and O'Leary (Bruce, 1999), in which the concept of information literacy was fully reflected in the type of skills that graduates require to perform competently within their professional capacities and as members of the community. The report outlines a profile of graduates leaving the university:

> Equipped with the skills and strategies to locate, access, retrieve, evaluate, manage and make use of information in a variety of fields, rather than with a finite body of knowledge that will soon be outdated and irrelevant. (CAUL, 2001: 14)

As a result of these initiatives, the information literacy framework was introduced in 2001 by CAUL. This was based on the American ACRL standards, which were adapted to suit the HE conditions in Australia. The Australian standards were approved by a CAUL meeting in October 2000 with the aim of applying them primarily within the HE environment. However, the future implementation of these standards by other educational sectors was also envisaged. Further collaborative work in this area between Australia and New Zealand led to the establishment of ANZIIL, which is responsible for the publication of a second edition of the Information Literacy Standards[28] in 2004 (Bundy, 2004). As a parallel development, the debate on information literacy was promoted by five national conferences[29] organised by the University of South Australia Library and the Australian Library and Information Association (ALIA). Bundy, who played a central role in this initiative, presents an account of the first four of these events (Bundy, 1999, 2001) to illustrate the steps taken by Australia in ensuring an effective exploration of the impact of information literacy on a number of sectors to develop a national implementation strategy. The first conference, Information Literacy: The Australian Agenda, in 1992, examined this concept from a national perspective, acknowledged some fundamental principles through aims that promoted information literacy 'as an essential competency for lifelong learning'[30] and stressed its value at individual and social levels. This event also established vital networks to support the collaborative initiatives promoting information literacy at national and cross-sectoral levels.[31] The 1992 conference set the parameters for a national agenda on information literacy, while the conference in 1995, Learning for Life: Information Literacy and the Autonomous Learner, identified information literacy as a 'key educational issue' (Bundy,

1996: 1) that should shape developments across the educational sectors and beyond to foster independent lifelong learning.[32] The third conference, in 1997, Information Literacy: The Professional Issue, shifted the focus of exploration to reflect different professional perspectives on information literacy and promote its dissemination to professional and accrediting organisations beyond those normally associated with these initiatives, such as library and information professionals. The fourth conference, in 1999, Concept, Challenge, Conundrum: From Library Skills To Information Literacy, explored the variance in the interpretation of this term by information practitioners,[33] examined the challenge of implementing information literacy to foster 'an information literate citizenry' (Bundy, 2000: 4), and reflected on the conundrum portrayed by the view that 'information literacy is not a library issue, although it is an issue for Librarianship' (ibid.: 5). Bundy argues that these considerations lead to the application of information literacy to suit wider social perspectives and to address the need to counteract the slow progress reflected by a dearth of information literacy initiatives in public libraries. The fifth conference, in 2001, Information Literacy: The Social Action Agenda, was the last event sponsored by the University of South Australia Library and ALIA, as the original goal of successfully integrating information literacy in professional practice had been successfully realised, and therefore the conferences had achieved what they had set out to accomplish. Being the last event in a series that spans ten years, this conference offered opportunities to reflect on the impact of the collaborative developments resulting from this forum, such as the creation of ANZIIL.

In her final editorial of the proceedings, Booker (2002) also identifies a number of direct benefits generated by this information literacy forum, including the achievement of international status by Australian information professionals as leading librarians in the provision of information literacy programmes and as leading researchers exploring the phenomenon from a range of perspectives.[34] Most importantly, however, information literacy education is fully endorsed by ALIA, and this approach, together with the fact that information literacy is no longer an unfamiliar term to librarians, drives this initiative forward. Bundy illustrates this point by quoting ALIA's statement on information literacy for all Australians, which describes it as an essential attribute for 'participative citizenship, social inclusion, the creation of new knowledge, personal empowerment and learning for life' (Bundy, 2002: 1). This statement illustrates the extent to which information literacy is prioritised by Australian information professionals, who promote it widely to cover all levels and sectors:

> Library and information services professionals therefore embrace a responsibility to develop the information literacy skills of their clients. They will support governments at all levels, and the corporate, community, professional, educational and trade union sectors, in promoting and facilitating the development of information literacy for all Australians as a high priority. (Ibid.)

National perspectives on information literacy in the UK

In the UK the information literacy debate focuses on the role of ICT in the HE sector. For example, the study by Creanor and Durndell (1994) on the impact of ICT in the period up to the early 1990s identified three main areas of influence that have determined the full integration of ICT strategies in HE. The study reported that:

- ICT was seen as the panacea to the expected increase in the number of students entering university, and the decreasing level of resources available to HE institutions. A decade later the government's e-learning strategy is still describing learning primarily in terms of the interaction with ICT. Such a position is criticised by professional bodies such as the CILIP, who raise a number of concerns including the fact that: 'Information literacy is never properly defined.[35]

- The introduction of ICT in the library system has transformed the way in which users gather information and requires a new approach to library instruction.

- The use of ICT has encouraged the adoption of innovative learning and teaching strategies such as resource-based learning and problem solving activities.

According to Hepworth (2000), since this study, provision has evolved from the implementation and assessment of ICT to the adoption of several forms of information literacy strategies in response to the demand for lifelong learning and transferable skills. These initiatives, he argues, have been introduced at subject level because the rapid expansion of the HE sector in the UK has meant that non-traditional students entering the university do not come equipped with the necessary independent learning skills required to engage with the innovative learning and teaching practices of problem-based and resource-based learning. Hepworth's findings are confirmed by the work of Ray and Day (1998) quoted by SCONUL (1999) in its paper on information skills to illustrate that the majority of students graduate without the necessary transferable skills required to cope with an information-based society. Similarly, the case studies in the third part of this book will show that information literacy provision at London Metropolitan University was introduced to counteract students' poor information-seeking and information-management skills as well as low competences in searching and evaluating learning resources.

From a national perspective, in September 1997 the Library and Information Commission (LIC) produced a discussion paper on a UK-wide information policy, which openly promoted the development of a universal information literacy strategy:

> A major effort is required to develop a base level of information literacy for everyone. The policy should set out a strategy for the achievement of this. It should encompass a wide range of skills, including numeracy, literacy, computer and information retrieval skills. It should also build on specific developments such as the wider introduction of information skills in the National Curriculum revisions for England, and proposals to teach thinking skills. It must be delivered at a variety of levels throughout the formal and informal education processes, and it should take advantage of the full range of delivery methods now available, including digital networks.[36]

Despite the recommendation by the LIC, the set of key skills identified by the *Dearing Report on Higher Education in the Learning Society* (1998) does not openly refer to information literacy competences. Instead, the report lists skills such as communication, numeracy, use of IT, learning how to learn and subject-specific skills. Although Dearing sees the ability to manage one's learning as a key skill 'in a society which needs increasingly to be committed to life-long learning' (Drew, 1998: 37), Town (2003) points out that the Dearing Report fails to make the crucial distinction between technology-related skills and information-related competences, in which the former falls within the skills-based literacy category, whereas the latter is associated with functional literacy, which Bawden and Robinson (2002: 297) describe as: 'the ability to read and use information essential for everyday life'.

In practice this has meant that a distinct approach to IT training was adopted through the European Computer Driving Licence (ECDL) route,[37] although no equivalent training programme has been developed for information literacy. Webber and Johnston (2000) confirm this bias towards ICT by quoting the key skills agenda as a recurrent theme found in the initiatives for HE and further education in the UK, where the focus rests entirely on ICT competences. For example, the National Grid for Learning, launched in 1998, identified ICT as key skills, whereas information literacy was omitted altogether. A similar bias is promoted by the DfES consultation paper *Towards a Unified E-Learning Strategy*,[38] in which e-learning is perceived as learning enhanced by the adoption of innovative strategies supported by information and communication technologies, but in which the skills required to enable such interaction are not fully articulated. In a comparison with other national information literacy initiatives Town comments that: 'This lack of a well-defined and accepted concept of information literacy in national policy and planning appears to be a key difference between the UK and other English-speaking countries' (Town, 2003: 89). As a result, the efforts of implementing an information literacy strategy lack much needed coordination at national level. This point is illustrated by SCONUL and is also confirmed by the findings of The Big Blue Project. SCONUL comments that although provision is widespread, 'much is left to the initiative and actions of small groups of interested staff [i.e. librarians and subject teachers], working in pockets and with no overall framework' (SCONUL, 1999: 8). The Big Blue Project (2001b), in its review of information literacy provision in the UK, states that 'there is no overarching cohesive strategy to information skills training in higher education in the UK [although] there are many examples of good practice'.[39]

The development and integration of information literacy initiatives in the UK HE sector is therefore driven by individual institutions and organisations operating within the educational environment. For example, in December 1999 SCONUL charged a task force with the responsibility of publishing a statement on *Information Skills in Higher Education* to 'stimulate debate about the place of information skills within the context of current activity surrounding 'key skills', 'graduate-ness' and lifelong learning' (SCONUL, 1999: 2). This is in contrast to developments in the USA and Australia, where the challenge of developing an information literacy policy is met by the accrediting professional bodies representing the wider community of library and information professionals, such as ALA and ALIA. There is evidence that CILIP was considering the development of an information literacy strategy in 2002; a report on CILIP's position on the knowledge economy put forward the following recommendations:[40]

- CILIP should develop a skills framework that reflects an information skills continuum, the context of the application of those skills, and a range of skills that enable effective application.

- CILIP should work with government and other bodies to ensure that basic information literacy skills become a core competence of all members of society – part of the national curriculum.

- CILIP should instigate further research into the utilisation and development of information literacy skills within the information continuum.

However, recent communication with CILIP illustrates that information literacy is not a policy priority: 'the Executive Advisory Groups that CILIP established were given a brief to explore possibilities in relation to the work/policy of CILIP. The recommendations they made did not themselves become policy – and there were a few that, although laudable, were beyond our scope/resources (both human and financial)'.[41] So far work in this area has consisted of a preliminary examination of the frameworks devised by ACRL, ANZIIL and SCONUL, which has led CILIP to conclude that these models do not suit the UK experience or are not fully transferable across all the library and information sectors that CILIP represents. However, some activities on the implementation of an information literacy strategy are in progress and operate at two levels. A small working group has been set up to assess the applicability of the Prague definition of information literacy, and place this in context by exploring the interpretations of information literacy used by practitioners in different sectors.[42] A long-term strategy is also in place and it is reflected in the work undertaken by the Community Services group, whose aim is to provide an audit of information literacy practices in order to collate 'scenarios'[43] that CILIP intends to use for dissemination purposes across the information sectors.

The technology-driven perspective is also illustrated by the focus adopted by the British eLit conference series, which explores the convergence of two main strands operating specifically in the educational environment. These are the IT and computer literacy strand contexualised within IT service and academic contexts, and the information skills/literacy strand based within library contexts.[44] The interaction between these two factors provided the focus of the First

International Conference on IT and Information Literacy, hosted jointly by Glasgow Caledonian University, the University of Glasgow and the University of Strathclyde in Glasgow in March 2002 (ibid.). The second conference was held in 2003 under the new title of eLiteracy.[45] By promoting e-learning, this conference narrowed its focus to explore the learning opportunities afforded specifically by electronic environments, thereby shifting the emphasis from information literacy to digital literacy, and supporting the view that in the UK information literacy is seen primarily from a technology-driven perspective. The digital literacy theme was perpetuated by the third conference on eLiteracy held in June 2004,[46] the focus of which offered further reflection on what it means to be eLiterate. The impact of this phenomenon on learning was assessed across all educational sectors and from the perspectives of a range of professionals, including library and faculty staff as well as IT support providers.[47] A recurring theme emerged in the IT and Information Literacy Conference in 2002 and the second eLiteracy event in 2003 regarding the challenges faced by faculty and library staff when attempting to collaborate on information literacy programmes. In her review of the 2002 conference, Webber (2003) summarises a number of these issues faced by academic librarians, who find that faculty staff express little interest in information literacy and are unwilling to allocated curriculum time to cover this. The comment by Smart (2003) on the eLit conference held in 2003 raises similar concerns by the library staff who participated in this event about having to sell information literacy to reluctant academics:

> Librarians still have an identity crisis which means we are still not wholly sure to which mast we should be nailing our colours – meanwhile the world moves relentlessly on. As someone at the 2003 Glasgow conference asked, where were the academics (the very people we need to convince) among the delegates, and are we in danger of ending up talking in a room among ourselves rather than to the people we need to convince about information literacy? At the very least, let's shore up those strategic alliances.

By contrast, Webber's review of the 2002 conference presents a different problem of collaboration experienced by faculty staff:

> Caroline Stern (Ferris State University) put forward the teacher's view: she had encountered librarians who discouraged academics

who wanted to include information literacy in the curriculum. (Webber, 2003)

There is an interesting comparison to be made between the concerns expressed by Stern and the problems of collaboration that librarians raise when attempting to implement information literacy initiatives. Stern's comment reflects the conditions in the USA where information literacy is seen as part of the faculty's responsibility, whereas in the UK this is perceived primarily as a library-driven initiative.

Summary

The literature depicts a shift from library education to information literacy within the HE environment in response to the challenges of lifelong learning and students' poor independent learning skills. This shift has generated its own challenges in terms of defining the elusive concept of information literacy and of adopting its learning-how-to-learn approach. In response to these challenges, the USA and Australia have integrated the information literacy approach within their national learning agenda by establishing, through legislation, a strong link between this strategy and the lifelong learning goal. This is complemented by the active role of the information professionals' organisations, which have helped to define this concept by promoting a debate at national level through a series of conferences, and have contributed to its integration within HE practices by setting up institutions on information literacy. The UK, by contrast, has chosen the technology-driven approach to develop its national learning agenda, in which ICT skills are prioritised and the independent learning approach is not fully defined. This is paralleled by CILIP's reluctance to develop and implement an information literacy policy that could offer the degree of coherence required for dissemination of this strategy at a national level.

Notes

1. Nanyang Technological University, Singapore.
2. Now called London Metropolitan University following a merger between the University of North London and London Guildhall University in August 2002.

3. Ferris State University in Big Rapids, Michigan, *http://www.ferris.edu* (accessed 18 April 2004). Stern's study surveyed 1184 students out of a yearly cohort of 2345.

4. The distinction between high and low order is also used by the information literacy frameworks developed by ACRL and ANZIIL and will be explored further in Chapter 3 of this book.

5. This approach is explored further in Chapter 4, in which the knowledge-spiral method is used for information literacy provision at postgraduate level.

6. The text here is an extract from the paper by Hepworth (2000: 24).

7. Bruce further defines these as library and IT skills.

8. Bruce here refers to lifelong learning skills, which are explored in Chapter 4 through the 'how one learns' perspective promoted by McInnis and Symes (1991).

9. Particularly in the HE environment.

10. A practical example of the learners' reflections is illustrated by the students' self-evaluative exercise examined by the first case study in Chapter 5.

11. *http://www.literacytrust.org.uk/* (accessed 22 April 2004).

12. *http://www.literacytrust.org.uk/* (accessed 22 April 2004).

13. Extract from Bundy (2004: 5).

14. The Big Blue Project was funded by the Joint Information Systems Committee through the JISC Committee for Awareness, Liaison and Training (JCALT) and was managed jointly by Manchester Metropolitan University Library and Leeds University Library.

15. The text in italics is a direct quote from the consultation paper: *Towards a Unified e-learning Strategy*. Department for Employment and Skills (DfES): 37. *http://www.dfes.gov.uk/consultations2/16/* (accessed 12 June 2004).

16. Quoted in Doherty et al. (1999), Boyer Commission on Educating Under-graduates in the Research University (1998), *Reinventing Undergraduate Education: a Blueprint for America's Research Universities*: 1–19.

17. The extract is from the Boyer Commission: 11.

18. Details of web-based information literacy initiatives run by American HE institutions can be found at: *http://www.ala.org/ala/acrl/acrlissues/acrlinfolit/infolitresources/infolitinaction/coursessyllabi.htm* (accessed 3 May 2004).

19. Formerly called the National Information Literacy Institute.

20. *http://www.infolit.org/index.html* (accessed 14 April 2004).

21. Oberman, C. The Institute for Information Literacy, footnote 1, *http://ala.org/acrl/iiltrain.html* (accessed 12 December 2002).

22. International Conference of Information Literacy Experts. The Prague Declaration: 'Towards an Information Literate Society', Prague, Czech Republic, September 2003, *http://www.infolit.org/International_Conference/index.htm* (accessed 15 April 2004).

23. The papers included in this chapter are taken from the educational group. Readers who wish to explore papers from other sectors can access these in full-text from: *http://www.nclis.gov/libinter/infolitconf&meet/grouppaper.html* (accessed 18 April 2004).

24. This is an extract of the Prague Declaration's Executive Summary: 1.

25. Mergers in this case have created institutions characterised by multi-campuses spanning hundreds of kilometres and supporting a larger number of students at a distance.
26. Also known as the Ross Report, which was commissioned by the Australian National Board of Employment, Education and Training in 1989 (CAUL, 2001).
27. The Committee advised the Australian Education Council and Ministers of Vocational Education, Employment and Training on Key Competencies for Employment Related Post-Compulsory Education and Training (1991–1992).
28. This document includes a detailed list of HE institutions in Australia that have implemented an information literacy policy based on the first edition of the *Information Literacy Standards*.
29. The proceedings for these conferences can be obtained from: Auslib Press, PO Box 622, Blackwood, South Australia 5051, Australia, e-mail: *info@auslib.com.au*.
30. One of the aims of the conference.
31. This led to the creation of the South Australian Forum for Information Literacy. Not surprisingly, Patricia Senn Breivik, the founding Chair of the National Forum on Information Literacy, was among the key speakers for this event.
32. At this event Eric Mayer raised some important issues in his opening speech that need to be addressed to ensure that the lifelong learning perspective is fully endorsed by the HE curricula. His view of lifelong learning is clearly articulated by the last question he posed: 'Is the interaction between learning and applying that learning a factor in curriculum development at all levels of education and training?' (Mayer, 1996: 5).
33. The ACRL Information Literacy Competency Standards for HE were also circulated at this event to elicit feedback from the participants.
34. Booker identifies the work of Bruce, *The Seven Faces of Information Literacy*, as an example of this.
35. The quote is from: *CILIP – Responses – DfES Consultation Towards a Unified e-learning Strategy*. A discussion between CILIP and Diana Laurillard, Head of the e-Learning Strategy Unit, DfES, at the London School of Economics Library, 13 January 2004, *http://www.cilip.org.uk/advocacy/responses/elearning2.html* (accessed 29 June 2004).
36. Library and Information Commission, *Keystone for the Information Age: a National Information Policy for the UK*, *http://www.lic.gov.uk/publications/policyreports/keystone.html*, last updated 16 March 1999 (accessed 14 April 2004).
37. The European Computer Driving Licence Foundation Ltd. (ECDL-F) *http://www.ecdl.com/main/index.php* (accessed 10 July 2004).
38. DfES Towards a Unified e-learning strategy, launched on 8 July 2003 *http://www.dfes.gov.uk/consultations2/16/* (accessed 19 May 2004).
39. One of these examples of good practice is provided by the collaborative work between SCONUL and the Open University (OU), which has resulted in a number of information literacy initiatives that have been fully integrated in the OU's curricula. These include SAFARI, a web-based resource that

develops generic information skills, MOSAIC, a self-contained information literacy unit (Dillon et al., 2003), *http://www.open.ac.uk/mosaic/index.cfm* (accessed 9 July 2004). Examples of Information Literacy programmes in the UK can be found at: *http://www.sconul.ac.uk/activities/inf_lit/links/ programmes.html* (accessed 27 September 2004).

40. Extract from the Report by the Executive Advisory Group (2002: 27).
41. Extract from e-mail communication with Cathy Ennis, Senior Adviser at CILIP's Department of Knowledge & Information, 2 July 2004.
42. The findings of this working group should in the public domain as of July 2004.
43. These information literacy contexts developed by CILIP would resemble the cases illustrated in the report produced by ALA, Presidential Committee on Information Literacy, 10 January 1989, Washington, DC: 2–3.
44. *http://www.elit-conf.org/itilit2002/index.html* (accessed 30 April 2004).
45. *http://www.elit2003.com/* (accessed 30 April 2004).
46. *http://www.elit-conf.org/elit2004/* (accessed 30 April 2004).
47. *http://www.elit-conf.org/elit/about.html* (accessed 30 June 2004). The 2005 eLit will be held at the University of Strathclyde in Glasgow, *http://www .elit-conf.org/index.html* (accessed 10 July 2004).

3

Comparison of the information literacy frameworks

> Understanding involves placing knowledge in a context. It requires determining how the information or data was produced, by whom, why, and whether or not it is relevant ... we know that ... information is not knowledge, that information retrieval is not research, that undergraduates cannot always evaluate websites. (Albrecht and Baron, 2002: 78)

This part of the book compares the three information literacy frameworks developed by ACRL, ANZIIL and SCONUL. The main themes arising from this comparison explored in this chapter include the strategies of integration of information literacy at institutional level, through the collaboration of faculty, library and administrative staff; and at subject and curriculum levels, through the articulation of learning outcomes and assessment practices that foster high-order thinking. Full copies of the three information literacy frameworks are included as appendices at the end of the book, but a summary of the main points of each is given in Table 3.1.

At a first glance all three models contain similar methods of processing the information, beginning with the identification of a need for information, followed by the methods of accessing and evaluating the information retrieved to answer the enquiry that initiated this process. A closer examination, however, reveals that there is a greater overlap between the standards offered by ACRL and ANZIIL.[1] These similarities are illustrated by overt features such as the sharing of the term 'information literacy' compared with SCONUL's use of the term 'information skills'. In terms of overlap, all three models address the issues related to the ethical use of information, although ANZIIL promotes the widest perspective on this by identifying social, cultural and economic aspects

Table 3.1	Summary of the three information literacy (IL) models

ACRL IL standards		ANZIIL IL standards		SCONUL information skills	
An information-literate person is able to:					
1	determine the extent of information needed	1	recognise a need for information and to determine the extent of information needed	1	recognise a need for information
2	access the required information effectively and efficiently	2	find information effectively and efficiently	2	distinguish ways in which the information gap may be addressed
3	evaluate information and its sources critically and incorporate selected information into his/ her knowledge base and value system	3	critically evaluate information and the information-seeking process	3	construct strategies for locating information
4	use information effectively to accomplish a specific purpose	4	manage information collected or generated	4	locate and access information
5	understand many of the economic, legal, and social issues surrounding the use of information, and access and use information ethically and legally	5	apply prior and new information to construct new concepts or create new understandings	5	compare and evaluate information obtained from different sources
6	–	6	use information with understanding and acknowledge cultural, ethical, economic, legal and social issues surrounding the use of information	6	organise, apply and communicate information to others in ways appropriate to the situation
7	–	7	–	7	synthesise and build upon existing inform-ation, contributing to the creation of new knowledge

of information ethics, whereas the other two frameworks emphasise the legal aspects of information use, such as copyright. Although ACRL promotes critical and evaluative thinking to increase the learner's knowledge-base, ANZIIL is the only one of these three frameworks that refers to knowledge-construction to describe the learning process that underpins information literacy education. SCONUL, by contrast, applies a hierarchical structure of knowledge acquisition, in which the creation of knowledge is perceived as the seventh and highest information literacy competence that can be achieved only by advanced learners, such as postgraduate students.

Overall the information literacy frameworks employed by ACRL and ANZIIL seem easier to apply because they start from the description of general information literacy standards, and expand on each one through the identification of performance indicators and of measurable learning outcomes that foster integration within subject-specific curricula. The ANZIIL framework, however, offers a more comprehensive pedagogical approach based on Bruce's three elements of learning, comprising experience, reflection and practice. In contrast with the other two frameworks, ANZIIL promotes a wider social dimension that enables its application beyond the confines of HE. The issues raised by these frameworks are examined in detail below, and, where appropriate, these are cross-referenced with the information literacy practice presented in the two case studies discussed in Chapters 5 and 6.

Application of the information literacy framework

ACRL presents three main premises associated with the use of its information literacy standards. First, learners are expected to acquire all of the information literacy competences, although ACRL acknowledges that the level of proficiency and the amount of time spent covering these skills will vary according to the abilities of individual learners. In addition, it recognises that emphasis on the mastery of specific competences is dictated by the nature and requirements of the discipline studied. A recursive performance of competences is expected to enable learners to evaluate the impact of, and to reflect on, the information-seeking activities to implement a revised and improved process of enquiry.

ANZIIL supports a similar view in stating that: 'the standards are not intended to represent a linear approach to information literacy' (Bundy,

Figure 3.1   Information literacy elements (Bundy, 2004: 7)

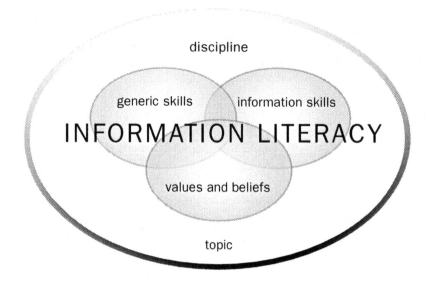

2004: 8). On the contrary, the acquisition of these competences operates on a process of reiteration. Similarly to the ACRL model, this framework also stresses the importance of contextualising information literacy within disciplinary curricula and that the relevance of the information literacy standards needs to be established according to the subject requirements in which these standards are applied. However, ANZIIL goes further in identifying three distinct dimensions of learning that constitute the framework of information literacy and that enable the application of this framework of learning within a wider social perspective (Figure 3.1):

- Generic skills described as: problem solving, collaboration, teamwork, communication and critical thinking.
- Information skills involving competences in: information seeking, information use and information technology fluency.
- Values and beliefs listed as: using information wisely and ethically, social responsibility and community participation (Bundy, 2004: 7).

By contrast, the SCONUL model of information skills is illustrated by a diagrammatic representation of a set of information competences structured into two main strands (Figure 3.2):

Figure 3.2   SCONUL information skills model (SCONUL, 1999: 7)[2]

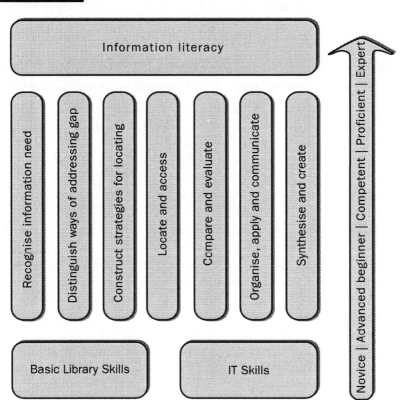

- The first strand describes a competent student who is able to function effectively as part of the academic community in terms of basic library and IT skills. Competences here refer to study skills and 'a tool for the job of being a learner' (SCONUL, 1999: 5). Included here are competences in the use of the library, performing literature searches and the use of citation and referencing systems that fulfils expectations of the tutors.[3]
- The second aspect, portrayed diagrammatically as seven pillars, is defined as information skills, although these are seen as interchangeable with information literacy, and include:

  awareness and understanding of the way in which information is produced in the modern world, critical appraisal of the content and validity of the information, some practical ideas of how information in the real world is acquired, managed, disseminated and exploited, particularly with knowledge of how appropriate professional groups use information in the workplace, in business and in the world of culture and the arts. (Ibid.)

The basic skills underpinning the SCONUL model are associated with specific information-related activities: 'At the base of the model are the twin fundamental building blocks of basic library skills and basic IT skills. The former is apparent in the user education programmes of academic libraries, the latter can be seen in developments such as the ECDL' (SCONUL, 1999: 7). By placing library and IT skills as foundations of the seven information literacy competences, SCONUL promotes the view that the latter can only be developed after the learner has mastered the basic set of skills and has become a competent information user. This distinction between the two strands sets the SCONUL model apart from the other two information literacy frameworks, which divide the levels of competence into two main categories: higher- and lower-order thinking. The SCONUL distinction replicates a false separation between technical and information literacy skills that is difficult to sustain in practice. Even when using basic systems of research such as the library online catalogue, or a search engine such as Google, students must be equipped with critical thinking skills, which SCONUL attributes to the more complex information literacy strand (Andretta, 2002).

Higher- and lower-order thinking

The ACRL information literacy standards cover the learning needs of students at all levels thanks to the distinction made between higher- and lower-order thinking skills.[4] Examples of activities associated with lower-order thinking skills include the identification of keywords, synonyms and related terms for the information required.[5] Higher-order thinking, by contrast, involves the accomplishment of a higher level of abstraction to develop a new hypothesis that may require additional information.[6] ANZIIL follows a similar strategy of fostering higher- and lower-order thinking, stresses the importance of assessing information literacy within the disciplinary content, and emphasises the need to use a range of assessments to develop different types of skills, knowledge and understanding set at different levels of complexity. A number of best assessment practices are identified, in which:

- information literacy is incorporated in the objectives and learning outcomes of units of study and assessment tasks;

- assessment is designed to structure and to sequence a complex task;

- assessment is planned and sequenced throughout the entire degree, providing a developmental framework. In addition, outcomes are listed to enable the monitoring of students' progression towards becoming information literate (Bundy, 2004: 27).

This approach ensures that the standards can be customised to fit institutional goals, subject requirements and level of complexity. Booth and Fabian (2002) provide concrete applications of the ACRL standards by illustrating how the learning outcomes are embedded in subject-specific contexts.[7]

Similarly to the view presented by both ALA and ANZIIL, SCONUL argues that expertise in information literacy competences is achieved through practice and reiteration. However, SCONUL makes a further distinction between the level of achievement and the number of competences that certificate-level students can attain compared with more advanced postgraduate students: 'The progression from novice to expert is indicated by an arrow. First year undergraduates will largely be at the bottom of the arrow, perhaps only practising the first four skills, while postgraduate and research students will aim to be towards the expert end, and will be aspiring to the seventh' (SCONUL, 1999: 7). As previously mentioned, the glass-ceiling imposed on first-year students separates SCONUL's information skills model from the other two frameworks, which put forward a more flexible distinction between higher- and lower-order thinking, while acknowledging that the development of these skills depends on the competences of individual learners. The view promoted by SCONUL is supported by Mellon's (1988) framework that maps students' cognitive development onto four stages. The initial stage of 'dualism' characterises the intellectual level of the majority of first-year undergraduate students. At this stage students expect a right or a wrong answer to each question they come across. Consequently, information skills can only be developed at a simple level, and the searching strategies taught should not contain too many different approaches in response to a specific problem. Mellon explains that this is because: 'Dualistic students have little patience with alternative search strategies ... all designed to answer the same type of question and with complexity of information retrieval' (Mellon, 1988: 80). As students move through the intellectual stages of 'multiplicity', 'relativism' and 'commitment' (ibid.: 80–1) they develop a more complex perception of the world. Here the learners engage with more sophisticated problem-solving tasks associated with elaborate concepts of retrieval and manipulation of information, and use these skills for a variety of situations, thus making their abilities truly transferable. As with the view promoted by SCONUL, this approach expects the last two stages of development to be accomplished by students who are in the final year of their degree or those in postgraduate education.

This perspective, however, is not always confirmed by practice, as the level of competences of each learner is not dictated by his or her academic status but by the individual learner's ability to engage with complex problem-solving conditions and their capacity for independent learning at the outset. Although the dualist approach manifests itself in the searching behaviour of first-year undergraduate students (Andretta, 2001, 2002), a recent study,[8] funded by the Learning and Teaching Support Network for Information and Computer Sciences (LTSN-ICS) in 2002/3, illustrates that such a demarcation of competences becomes blurred when the information literacy skills of students at more advanced level are examined. Initially this study focused on the development of a web-based information literacy programme for dissertation students studying for a BSc in information management. However, the use of this site was expanded to support postgraduate dissertation students exhibiting poor information literacy competences to help them improve their independent learning skills (Andretta, 2004). The findings from this research therefore indicate that even at postgraduate level students may be unable to move beyond the dualist stage.

Information literacy is not synonymous with 'IT'

All three models are unanimous in the view that information literacy is a broader concept than IT literacy and IT fluency. ACRL and ANZIIL suggest that information literacy is an intellectual framework for 'understanding, finding, evaluating, and using information-activities which may be accomplished in part by fluency with IT, in part by sound investigative methods, but most important, through critical discernment and reasoning' (ACRL, 2000: 3). The SCONUL paper elaborates further on the difference between IT and information skills by claiming that the former includes the application of basic manipulation skills, such as keyboard use, mouse control, the use of standard word-processing and spreadsheet software, and the interaction with network applications such as e-mail, web and Internet browsing. Information skills, by contrast, consist of more complex competences covering the use of information sources, evaluation, manipulation and presentation strategies as well as navigational methods.

Information literacy models of integration

All three models propose full integration of information literacy practices within subject-specific curricula, although ANZIIL elaborates further on this by promoting the view that information literacy requires a sustained development at all levels of formal education, so that throughout their academic career students are exposed to 'repeated opportunities for seeking, evaluating, managing, and applying information gathered from multiple sources and obtained from discipline specific research methods'. (Bundy, 2004: 6). In addition, ANZIIL's framework offers a detailed description of the different levels of information literacy provision (ibid.). These levels are divided into:

- generic – extracurricular classes and/or self-paced packages;
- parallel – extracurricular classes and/or self-paced packages that complement the curriculum;
- integrated – classes and packages that are part of the curriculum;
- embedded – curriculum design in which students have ongoing interaction and reflection with information.

The embedded model is the most effective as it covers the three elements of learning involved in the information literacy process promoted by Bruce (2002):

- experiencing information literacy (learning);
- reflection on experience (being aware of learning);
- application of experience to novel contexts (transfer of learning).

A similar approach is illustrated by Doherty et al. (1999), whose paper presents the practice of Montana State University (MSU) libraries where three methods of provision are adopted:

- Discipline specific: in which basic library instruction is given to support writing classes.

- Course-specific instruction: which consists of advanced sessions on higher-level research concepts such as controlled vocabulary and citation technique.

- Credit classes: which emphasise critical thinking and information literacy skills by:

  > developing skills to determine information need; finding information appropriate to need, regardless of format; and evaluating the usefulness of the information for a given situation ... one of our goals is to create students with ... a critical attitude towards every piece of information they encounter. (Ibid.)

The third approach is based on the main goal of ensuring that students become information literate. Critical thinking is seen as a crucial element of this, and is supported by the need to establish an ownership of the learning by the students. To be critical thinkers, students also need to be reflective learners, i.e. they need to reflect on what they have learned and what remains to be covered.[9]

Information literacy multilevel integration

Both ANZIIL and ACRL argue that their information literacy frameworks can operate at a number of levels:

- At institutional level, where they offer guidance for policy development within subjects and professions, and provide evaluation strategies needed to assess the effectiveness of information literacy programmes. Booth and Fabian (2002) stress the importance of integrating information literacy within the institution's mission, goals and IT initiatives. With regard to integration, the CHE considers that an institution-wide approach is required. This is accomplished by identifying information literacy as an 'educational goal' (CHE, 1995: 5) to illustrate the full institutional commitment for this initiative and to ensure the allocation of appropriate resources to facilitate its implementation at campus-wide and cross-disciplinary levels.

- At programme level to frame curriculum objectives, learning outcomes and assessment criteria. The CHE questions the validity of information literacy as a stand-alone course following the injunction that 'Information literacy ... transcend disciplines ... enabling students to transfer basic skills from one specific disciplinary concept to another. Therefore, many institutions have found that information literacy is best integrated widely into curricula and its relevance reinforced at every point in the learning experience' (CHE, 1994: 10).

- At student level as it gives learners an awareness of the importance of information literacy, although both ACRL and ANZIIL acknowledge that coverage of the standards and level of competence achieved by each learner will vary according to subject requirements and students' abilities. In relation to motivating the students, the CHE argues that most importantly 'students must "buy into" the importance of information literacy in their own lives, and they are more likely to do so if they perceive its relevance to their future success and understand what they must do to become prepared as lifelong learners' (CHE, 1994: 13). The success of information literacy delivery also depends on the level of flexibility that characterises provision to take into account the high levels of variations in the students' information literacy skills at the point of entry.

SCONUL also argues that information skills must be integrated into the subject curriculum through the application of the following elements of good practice:[10]

- cater appropriately for all kinds of learners at all the various levels of learning;
- have clear aims and are based on sound pedagogical foundations;
- have quality and feedback mechanisms built in;
- attempt to measure initial and final competence (to demonstrate impact);
- are managed and delivered cost-effectively;
- make valid use of new technology and other innovations.

Information literacy: an institution-wide initiative

The view that collaboration between library, faculty and administrative staff is crucial to ensure the development of a coherent information literacy policy in any institution is fully promoted by the three models. This perspective envisages an active role for library and faculty staff who are expected to encourage students to develop independent learning skills through flexible provision of the learning resources. The work by Griffiths University in Australia is used by SCONUL as an example of good practice in developing an information literacy strategy, in which:

> Information Literacy education is the shared responsibility of all educators and information providers ... Effective information literacy education depends upon co-operation between information specialists and discipline experts to achieve curriculum innovations which foster information literacy. (Bainton, 2001: 9)

ACRL and ANZIIL expand the scope of this collaboration to an institution-wide context by allocating some responsibility for information literacy education to the administrative apparatus found in HE institutions. Here they argue that the role of administrative staff covers the planning and budgeting of information literacy programmes as well as the organisation of any staff development programme required in support of the introduction and long-term implementation of information literacy initiatives. A practical example of the extent of collaboration required is illustrated by the Information Literacy IQ (Institutional Quotient) test designed by Oberman and Wilson, which is freely available from the ACRL website.[11] This questionnaire was used at a seminar on information literacy organised by the Yorkshire Universities Information Skills group in June 2004,[12] where participants were asked to assess their institutions' capacity for information literacy provision. In a group of approximately 50 participants representing a number of academic institutions none could claim the status of a model programme achieved with a score of 12 points or above. At London Metropolitan University, collaboration supporting information literacy education involves a number of staff from faculty and library and from the administrative apparatus, including:

- faculty staff who are directly responsible for the development and delivery of the programmes;
- library staff who play an advisory role as well as contributing to the delivery of the syllabus;
- staff from the marketing department who operate the software that collates and analyses the data from the diagnostic questionnaire;
- Internet and IT support staff who are responsible for assembling the diagnostic questionnaire into a web-based interactive test.

It is important to note, however, that this example of collaboration is based on the good will of the staff involved, and that the frameworks promote a model of cooperation that is fully and officially integrated in the support apparatus available to sustain information literacy provision.

Summary

A comparison between these three frameworks has highlighted a common process of information literacy that reflects the definition originally proposed by ALA, involving the initial acknowledgement of the need for information, followed by competences in locating, evaluating and using that information effectively. The main difference rests on the emphasis placed by ANZIIL and ACRL on the recursive knowledge construction approach, which provides a coherent framework for learning. SCONUL's interpretation of the knowledge-creation process is too linear to reflect fully the learners' experience as it is based on a sequential progression from the foundation library and IT skills through the development of the seven competences, culminating in the creation of new knowledge at the highest level of the learning ladder.

All three frameworks agree in the promotion of an integrated information literacy strategy based on full collaboration between library and faculty staff, although ACRL and ANZIIL add the support by the administrative apparatus as a further component to this collaborative approach to ensure that the information literacy initiative operates within the institution as a whole. Grafstein argues that the promotion of a campus-wide information literacy strategy raises an important point about who is responsible for its implementation. She quotes the report by the CHE on information literacy, which claims that this initiative is clearly extended outside the library sphere of responsibility: 'information literacy is not the unique and sole province of librarians or other information providers, but it is an integral part of the objectives for every course on campus, and it requires administrative support for effective implementation' (Grafstein, 2002: 198). This point was first presented by Bundy (2000), who argued that information literacy is an issue for the library but not of the library. This perspective reinforces the claim presented here that information literacy has a wider pedagogical role to play compared with its predecessor, library education. Snavely notes that this issue was explored by ACRL's task force during the development of its information literacy standards. The task force concluded that: 'information literacy isn't just a library issue, but is an issue for all of higher education and society as well' (Snavely, 2001: 2). The view that information literacy transcends disciplines by fostering transferable skills needs to be endorsed at institutional level, and in the context of the two case studies in Chapters 5 and 6, this perspective is articulated at the level of individual module provision.

Notes

1. This is not surprising, given that ANZIIL's framework was originally developed from the ACRL standards.
2. In July 2004 the model was redesigned and renamed 'The Seven Pillars of Information Literacy model'. However, at the time of the editing of the model, SCONUL's position paper on Information Skills remained unchanged. PDF and GIF versions of this new model are available at: *http://www.sconul.ac.uk/activities/inf_lit/sp/model.html* (accessed 20th September 2004).
3. Identified by Webber and Johnston (2003) as the expert mode of assessment discussed in Chapter 4 of this book.
4. These are based on the Bloom taxonomy of educational objectives.
5. Chapter 5 will illustrate provision of this approach at certificate level of the social science undergraduate scheme.
6. Higher-order thinking is strongly associated with independent investigation and is therefore employed at postgraduate level through the research methods module, which is explored in Chapter 6 of this book. However, the knowledge construction approach based on the principles of reiteration and reflection underpins provision at certificate level as well, although in this case a step-by-step approach is used to facilitate the learning process.
7. Details of these examples are given in Appendix D.
8. Andretta, S., information literacy website designed to develop information handling competences for undergraduate information management students. *http://www.ics.ltsn.ac.uk/devfund/Susie_Andretta.html* (accessed 26 May 2004).
9. The diagnostic questionnaire used for information literacy provision at certificate level, explored by the first case study, operates according to this principle.
10. Extract from Bainton (2001: 9).
11. *http://www.ala.org/ala/acrl/acrlissues/acrlinfolit/professactivity/iil/immersion/infolitiqtest.htm* (accessed 7 July 2004). This is included in Appendix E.
12. The event was entitled: 'Information skills teaching: does it work?' and was organised by the Yorkshire University Libraries, 21 June 2004, and hosted by Leeds Metropolitan University, UK.

4

Information literacy practice

> Effective information users will be generalists, people who can tease knowledge and understanding out of large information flows. They will be pattern finders, applying new intellectual skills and working with more powerful information tools. (Ford, 1995: 99)

Chapters 2 and 3 of this book identify the issues associated with information literacy and provide a framework of standards that can be used to integrate this strategy within an HE institution. The remainder of the book turns its focus to the actual practice of information literacy implemented by the staff from the Information Management School in the Department of Applied Social Sciences (DASS), London Metropolitan University.[1] These concrete examples of information literacy education take the form of case studies, which reflect on the impact of this provision on the students from the perspective of the information literacy educator. This approach provides a more holistic picture of what it means to practise information literacy through the fostering of independent learning in the students, and through continuous reflection on practice by the educator, as advocated by Schön (1991) and O'Brien (1998).

This chapter discusses three principal issues associated with information literacy education that have a bearing on the practice of the case studies presented in Chapters 5 and 6:

- the emergence of a new learning culture;
- the role of the tutor within this innovative learning environment;
- the assessment strategies that foster reflection on the learning process.

Once this pedagogical context is set two different models of information literacy integration addressing diverse subject requirements and levels of provision will be explored. These cases adopt the embedded and integrated approaches as defined by ANZIIL's categories of integration explored in Chapter 3.[2] The literature makes a more general distinction between two types of information literacy provision: 'stand-alone' and 'curriculum-integrated' modules. (Booth and Fabian, 2002: 124). If this dual model is used, then the two case studies would subscribe to the curriculum-integrated approach, where information literacy operates in a multidisciplinary environment, and where provision is based on close partnership between faculty and library staff (Breivik, 1998), supported by the administrative apparatus (ACRL, 2000; Bundy, 2004). Such a strategic alliance is essential according to Rockman (2002: 185) 'to establish information literacy as a foundation for student learning'. The two case studies show how information literacy integration into the curriculum is applied at undergraduate certificate[3] level, through a department-wide information literacy module, and at postgraduate level through the delivery of the Applied Information Research (AIR) module, which is part of the MA in Information Services Management.[4] In the certificate level module, the syllabus is based on the general information literacy definition devised by ALA[5] and on the SCONUL information skills model, whereas in AIR information literacy is embedded within a research skills context and is aimed at fostering lifelong learning attitudes (ANZIIL, 2004). Here the information literacy skills paradigm is implemented from the perspective of the 'reflective practitioner' (Schön, 1991), and the action research perspective as recommended by O'Brien (1998) and by Moore (2002).

The employment of transferable skills associated with the information literacy and the independent learning initiatives is fully promoted through information literacy practice in DASS in accordance with Bruce's view that the effects of provision should go beyond the academic sphere: 'In both undergraduate and postgraduate education there is an ongoing challenge to ensure that experiences gained in the academic environment are transferable to professional and other contexts' (Bruce, 1997: 10).

Information literacy: a lifelong learning culture

King describes the traditional lecture and note-taking scenario as the 'transmittal mode' of learning (King, 1993: 30) based on the assumption that students are empty containers receiving knowledge transmitted by the tutor. Such a passive learning approach is outdated and inadequate to address the challenges of developing lifelong learning competences, which can only be achieved through a constructivist approach. This is based on the premise that:

> Knowledge is a state of understanding and can only exist in the mind of the individual [learner]; as such, knowledge must be constructed – or reconstructed by each learner through the process of trying to make sense of new information in terms of what that individual already knows. (Bruce, 1997: 10)

This process leads to the creation of new ideas generated by the interaction between the new information and the existing knowledge. Unlike the transmittal mode, the constructivist approach fosters a student-centred perspective within a learning environment characterised by problem-solving activities (Bruce, 1997), in which the learners 'make meanings for themselves' (King, 1993: 30) by interacting with subject-specific information. First-year students in DASS, for example, develop searching and evaluative skills through a series of problem-based interactive tutorials, while at postgraduate level information literacy competences support a more complex investigative process embedded in real world conditions that are reflected in the articulation of a research proposal in the form of an application for funding.

McInnis and Symes highlight the shift in educational perspectives in which a distinction is made between the role played by the discipline taught and that played by the learning process in its own right: 'while some believe that education is to provide students with a world to understand, others believe that the purpose of education is to help students develop ways to understand the world'. (McInnis and Symes, 1991: 225). They conclude that the focus is shifting from 'what one learns [to] how one learns' (ibid.). This view promotes a greater emphasis on the process of learning that fosters the development of transferable skills, rather than concentrating on the accomplishment of a specific task. The 'how one learns' perspective is complemented by what Bruce describes as a shift in teaching practices from content to process orientation, in which the amount of content learned is no longer of primary importance, but the ability to learn is. As a result, information literacy should be promoted: 'as a vehicle of enhancing critical enquiry and self-directed learning and as a foundational element of a broader focus on lifelong learning' (Bruce, 2002: 12). The lifelong learning approach is central to information literacy provision in DASS, which strongly promotes the transferability of these skills. For example, the two modules presented by the case studies cover the process of searching by requiring the formulation and construction of a search. This can be applied to query a range of information systems and, therefore, such a strategy is transferable to any information-seeking activity required to fulfil academic and work-related tasks. Student feedback in the first case study illustrates that they are very aware of the transferability factor of this module, and take advantage of this by using information literacy skills to complete other assignments. The issue of transferability was first raised by the students during the piloting of this undergraduate module in the academic year 2000/01. On completion of the pilot, the feedback from the students showed that the ICT assignment, which consisted of tests from the ECDL course-ware, did not offer the opportunity to apply the skills acquired through the ECDL tutorials. To replace the ECDL tests, a portfolio of ICT tasks was introduced that required students to apply a range of skills covered by the ECDL syllabus (Andretta and Cutting, 2003). The level and extent of transferability of the research skills developed by the postgraduate AIR module is documented by the students' feedback, presented in the second case study. The comments generated at the end of AIR suggest that skills learned in this module are transferred to support academic studies and further professional development.

Grafstein (2002) argues that at a general level information literacy skills need to cover the subject-specific knowledge-base as well as develop broader research-based principles that can be applied across the disciplines. Bruce and Candy expand on this view by promoting Bigg's principle of 'constructive alignment' (Bruce, 1999: 3), where information literacy educators must structure learning activities that encourage students to engage with content determined by the discipline through the process of effective information use. This approach is particularly effective when information literacy is integrated within subject-specific domains. In the first case study the students are encouraged to research a topic for an assignment from their own discipline, and this provides the incentive to interact with the sources of information and the learning process. At postgraduate level, information use is embedded within research practices that address the needs of information professionals. Subject integration is accomplished here by promoting information literacy as a way of learning through the research route in accordance with Bruce's claim that this framework can be applied across the disciplines: 'information literacy, like phenomena such as teaching and learning, does not have a life of its own, rather it is a way of thinking and reasoning about aspects of subject matter' (Bruce, 2002: 12). Similarly, Grafstein argues that in an academic environment characterised by disciplines whose boundaries are constantly expanding, the process of research is more important than the product:

> Emphasis should therefore be placed on the process of locating and retrieving information because these are the skills that students will need and that will facilitate their ability to acquire new information as the need arises. (Grafstein, 2002: 200)

Practice in DASS is based on information literacy as a framework of learning, although Bruce (2002) points out that the association between information literacy, lifelong learning and continuing professional development (CPD) is fully articulated only within the postgraduate level of provision.[6]

It is evident from the literature (Orr et al., 2001; Moore, 2002; Martin, 2003) that the creation of an information literacy learning culture requires a major shift in the educational paradigm and that, as a result, this new approach to learning and teaching may come into conflict with existing academic practices and expectations held by students and educators alike. The first challenge arises with the attempt to define what it means to be information literate. Bruce (2002) identifies a number of essential components for an information literacy programme. These include a curriculum that covers appropriate information literacy skills, fosters active engagement with the information environment, encourages reflection and documentation of learning about effective information practices, and finally enables the application of experience to new contexts; in other words, it enables the transfer of learning. However, Shapiro and Hughes question the actual translation of information literacy education into curricular activities and describe a range of interpretations that can be applied to shape an information literacy programme:

> Should everyone take a course in creating a web page, computer programming, TCP/IP protocols or multimedia authoring? Or are we looking at a broader and deeper challenge – to rethink our entire educational curriculum in terms of information? (Shapiro and Hughes, 1996: 1)

The case studies explored here offer ways of interpreting the information literacy at certificate level through the use of the general information literacy principles of locating, evaluating and using the information effectively for a given task, as defined by ALA's perspective, and through the development of fundamental research skills, such as library and ICT skills, prescribed by SCONUL. At postgraduate level, the emphasis rests on the 'knowledge spiral' approach advocated by Bawden and Robinson (2002: 298), in which the investigative process relies on complex critical thinking and reflective competences operating at the knowledge-construction and knowledge-extension ends of the learning spectrum (Bruce, 1997).

From a student perspective the challenges of becoming information literate rest on a number of factors. Ennis touches on one of these challenges by depicting students' expectations for: 'bite-sized chunks of information that have been pre-digested and regurgitated as a leaflet/booklet/study pack (paper and electronic equivalents)' (Ennis, 2001: 292). This point restates the problem of spoon-feeding found particularly during the provision of information literacy at certificate level of the undergraduate scheme at DASS. Practice there has shown the students' over-reliance on the tutor's guidance in the exploration of the subject knowledge and that, as a result, when faced with provision that encouraged independent learning the students experienced a deep sense of confusion reflected in the 'what do I do now?' attitude (Andretta, 2002: 121). This problem was particularly prominent during the first few weeks of the module, and not surprisingly, this inhibited the students's interaction with the learning resources. Feedback from the students at the end of the module confirmed that the expectations of spoon-feeding were not fully eradicated. The cohort in 2000/1, for example, associated compulsory attendance with a regular working pattern and increased learning[7] (Andretta and Cutting, 2003: 206). The first case study explores the plug-and-play strategy used to address this problem and assesses the impact of using formative diagnostic testing to help students take responsibility for their learning.

The role of the tutor: 'from the sage on the stage to the guide on the side'

According to Bundy '[the] traditional role [of the educator] as the fount of all knowledge will change because of the information explosion.

Learning will be less about knowledge residing in the head and more about learning the pathways to knowledge' (Bundy, 2001: 4). This is a fundamental principle underpinning the information literacy practices in DASS, where emphasis is placed on the students' competences to access and evaluate information that guides their investigations in subject-specific contexts. In this learning environment, the role of the tutor shifts from the 'sage on the stage [to] the guide on the side' (King, 1993: 30). As a facilitator the tutor is 'still responsible for presenting the course material, but he or she presents that material in ways that make the students do something with the information – interact with it – manipulate the ideas and relate them to what they already know' (ibid.). Facilitation of learning is essential in ensuring the transition from 'transmission of information to construction of meaning' (ibid.). Doherty et al. fully support the 'guide on the side' perspective as they challenge the academic belief that: 'The professors have the truth and students must swallow it. We remove ourselves as the "sage on the stage", thus de-emphasising the role of the instructor as yet another infallible source of information' (Doherty et al., 1999). They promote teaching methods that foster critical thinking and reflective skills generated by the level of scrutiny and investigative process applied by the students.

The following extract illustrates an example of the 'the guide on the side' approach generated by information literacy practice in DASS. The e-mail communication between a first-year undergraduate student and the tutor shows that the student is having difficulties with the formulation of a search topic required to complete one of the assignments for the Information Literacy module at certificate level. Initially the student is expecting the tutor to assess the suitability of the topic, as the student's efforts to engage with this process have been unsuccessful. The tutor's reply, however, does not comply with the student's request to cast a final judgment on the topic, as this would simply reinforce the student's dependence on the authority of the tutor. Instead, the tutor raises a number of questions about the topic to encourage the student's reflection on the process of narrowing down the focus of the research. The student engages with the questions by clarifying the terminology used, successfully narrows down the topic, and evaluates the appropriateness of the search without further help from the tutor.

> *Student*: I would be grateful if you could clarify whether this subject is suitable or not: 'Obtaining a visa to reside in the USA'. I have gone through the criteria for Internet research and I have given it a lot of thought with little success.
>
> *Tutor*: This is a vast subject. For example, a visa can have a number of purposes. Are you talking about short-term holiday visas or a visa to live in the States? This would already narrow your topic down. Also, what nationality were you thinking of? I am sure that the USA operates an immigration policy that varies according to country. Once you have addressed these issues then get back to me with a topic.
>
> *Student*: Thank you for responding. For clarity when I say 'reside' I am referring to living in the USA rather than a short stay. I didn't specifically say British as we were asked to use the Google search engine for the UK so I thought it might only bring up information appropriate to residents in the UK: 'British citizens obtaining a visa to reside in the USA'. The above is more specific [and] would be of better use for a search.
>
> *Tutor*: This is much better and clearer.

In parallel with the changed role of the tutor, the mode of delivery also changes:

> from the dominant paradigm of pre-packaging information for students in the form of textbooks, lectures, and even artificially constrained multimedia resources, to facilitating active learning using real world information resources. (Bruce, 2002: 5)

However, Doherty et al. (1999) concede that the traditional methods of delivery such as lectures can be appropriate as long as these are identified as the most suitable pedagogical tool rather than selected as the default.

Information literacy and assessment practices

In a review of assessment strategies associated with information literacy provision Webber and Johnston (2003) explore a number of factors that need to be taken into account when testing the effectiveness of information literacy programmes. They propose that assessment practices in this area should address the following purposes: diagnostic testing, formative and summative feedback, and quality assurance evaluation. Ideally, a combination of these strategies should be used to test different aspects of information literacy skills, and the case studies in Chapters 5 and 6 combine these approaches to provide a comprehensive evaluation of the impact of information literacy delivery, although practice at DASS has shown that diagnostic testing is a more effective method of integration at undergraduate level of provision, whereas formative and summative assessments are more appropriate at postgraduate level. The relevance of these strategies is fully explored in the case studies; however, some findings from these practices are worth mentioning at this point:

- *Diagnostic testing.* The most common strategies consist of quantitative assessment techniques involving pre- and post-tests, questionnaires and surveys (Lawson, 1999; Andretta, 2001; Knight, 2002). The pre-test and post-test approaches are preferred because they provide quantitative data on the students' learning profile and the consequent impact of the information literacy programme by evaluating students' information literacy skills on entry and by assessing the improvement of these competences on completion of the course (Lawson, 1999).[8] Diagnostic testing is used at certificate level in DASS to provide students with an individualised learning profile that identifies areas of weaknesses on which they need to concentrate. Practice has also shown that this approach increases students' motivation to engage with the learning resources.

- *Formative and summative feedback.* The formative strategy refers to continuous feedback given during the programme of study, which can be linked to formal assessment, or can simply provide feedback as a result of a non-assessed activity. Summative feedback, by contrast, is linked to assessment strategies that occur at the end of the programme of study. Information literacy provision at postgraduate level has shown that students' motivation to engage with formative activities is greater if these have a direct impact on the final grade awarded. It is therefore essential to emphasise the benefits of formative assessment, and in particular, to stress the impact of this on the overall assessed performance to encourage student engagement in this process.

- *Quality assurance evaluation.* Webber and Johnston (2003) identify two types of measurement for this purpose, namely student performance and overall progression data. Practice at DASS has led to the introduction of an additional criterion generated by the students' feedback illustrating reflection on their learning experience. This type of qualitative data complements the quantitative approach promoted by performance and progression rates because it provides details of the context in which information literacy operates, and offers a greater insight on the students' perception of the transferable aspect of information literacy skills. These points are explored in the analysis of the self-evaluation reports included in Chapter 5.

Webber and Johnston (2003) also distinguish between two assessment modes commonly used in HE:[9] the expert mode, which fosters surface learning, where information literacy is assessed through the use of tests which are then marked by the tutor/librarian (or expert); and the self-assessment mode, which requires some form of student self-evaluation about their learning progress. The latter fosters reflection and is associated with deep learning. However, the authors warn that often this mode is used without giving the students the support they need before the self-assessment exercise, and without offering appropriate feedback on completion of the reflective process. This lack of support, they argue, results in the students over-estimating the skills developed. Practice in DASS confirms that students require a great deal of support when attempting to reflect on their learning as they are not familiar with self-evaluation practices. This is particularly true of students at certificate level and the first case study illustrates ways of providing effective support to foster the students' reflective skills.

The portfolio is an assessment method commonly associated with information literacy education, where students' information literacy competences are ascertained through performance-based tasks. However, a combination of both diagnostic and competence-based assessment methods is useful because: 'tests may measure how well students have learned information, but they may not demonstrate how well students can solve problems using that information' (Rockman, 2002: 193). The assessment strategies adopted by the certificate-level module, for example, are based on both a diagnostic test as a formative form of assessment and on a summative assignment consisting of a portfolio of tasks that exposes students to a range of problem-solving activities involving interaction with a number of information systems. Most of the tasks in the portfolio are assessed through the expert mode, although student self-assessment is encouraged by providing good and bad examples for each task, produced by previous cohorts. The portfolio also includes a self-reflective activity, which provides the following benefits:

- it enables students to evaluate their progress on completion of the information literacy programme;
- it provides a clear profile of information literacy skills by the cohort that feeds into the revision of the information literacy syllabus;
- it offers information-rich data on the contextualisation and transferability factors associated with the information literacy skills.

The development of reflective skills is seen by Mutch as essential for effective information use and the adoption of a lifelong learning attitude:

> The lack of such reflective processes has been held to prevent a person from being able to respond to changed circumstances with new approaches. This suggests that a key to the effective use of information is not only a conscious recognition of the relationship with knowledge but also a critical awareness of the factors surrounding knowledge. (Mutch, 1997: 386)

Rockman also argues that it is important to emphasise the positive impact of information literacy through enhancement of the students' learning experience, the empowerment of students with a renewed confidence in learning, improving student motivation and 'providing a strong foundation for the retention and transferability of learning to any new experience' (Rockman, 2002: 190). With this in mind, the feedback from the self-reflective task presented in the first case study has also been used to inform new students about the comments made by previous cohorts. This approach reinforces the usefulness of the information literacy skills and their applicability to other learning contexts, particularly within the academic environment. At postgraduate level, by contrast, the perspective of the reflective practitioner is used to promote the reiterative process of information literacy, and its impact is explored in the second case study.

To ensure an effective contextualisation of information literacy, Snavely (2001) advocates collaboration between library and faculty to generate assessment strategies for information literacy that are appropriate to subject-specific contexts. In particular, assessment methods should be performance-based, and focus on the research process. This is especially relevant for information literacy educators who are urged to teach the research process and its concepts rather than simply to introduce electronic tools and technology to their users. Such a view reiterates the arguments supporting a move away from the library education approach presented in part one of this book, in which the emphasis rests on the provision of stand-alone programmes offering induction to facilities confined to the library environment and devoid of subject relevance.

Notes

1. London Metropolitan University will be referred to from now on as the University and the Department of Applied Social Sciences as DASS.
2. Extract from the models of integration promoted by the Australian and New Zealand information literacy framework. (ANZIIL): 'Embedded: curriculum design where students have ongoing interaction and reflection with information. Integrated: classes and packages that are part of the curriculum' (Bundy, 2004: 6).
3. Certificate level in the UK is synonymous with first year of an undergraduate degree.
4. This programme is accredited by the Chartered Institute of Library and Information professionals (CILIP), *http://www.cilip.org.uk/* (accessed: 8 June 2004). The information literacy programme here addresses the needs of the postgraduate students and fosters skills that are relevant to the information profession as a whole.
5. 'To be information literate, a person must be able to recognize when information is needed and have the ability to locate, evaluate, and use effectively the needed information'. Extract from ALA's report (1989).
6. In the Applied Information Research module the information literacy perspective is particularly relevant for the students as learners, by becoming effective information consumers and lifelong learners, and as information professionals, by becoming effective information producers/providers.
7. The spoon-feeding expectation is reinforced by practices elsewhere in the department, where attendance, recorded through attendance registers, is compulsory and poor performance is anecdotally associated with a poor attendance record.
8. The issue of quantifying the impact of information literacy provision was the focus of discussion at a seminar on 'information skills teaching: does it work?' referred to in Chapter 3. This event reflected the preoccupation by library professionals operating within the HE environment in the UK with the generation of evidence, such as improved student results, that would help promote information literacy programmes to faculty staff.
9. Webber and Johnston also identify the peer-assessment mode as an approach suitable for information literacy education. This method is not often associated with information literacy programmes in HE, but is a preferred practice within organisations that aim to sustain their competitive advantage through collaborative learning.

Case study 1: Information literacy module for social sciences

Information literacy, therefore, is a means of personal empowerment. It allows people to verify or refute expert opinion and to become independent seekers of truth. It provides them with the ability to build their own arguments and to experience the excitement of the search for knowledge ... It is unfortunate that the very people who most need the empowerment inherent in being information literate are the least likely to have learning experiences which will promote these abilities. Minority and at-risk students, illiterate adults, people with English as a second language, and economically disadvantaged people are among those most likely to lack access to the information that can improve their situations. (ALA, 1989)

This case study starts with an outline of the information literacy module delivered at the University during the academic year 2003/4. This provision demonstrates the implementation of an information literacy syllabus suitable for the certificate level of a range of social science undergraduate courses. The principle of a plug-and-play structure is explored to illustrate how this encourages students' active engagement with the learning process through the use of a formative diagnostic questionnaire, and a self-evaluation task completed at the end of the module. Themes raised by students' self-evaluation are examined through a qualitative analysis, which illustrates how information literacy skills are perceived by the learners on completion of the module, and provide evidence of skills' transferability to other modules.[1] Ongoing developments of information literacy provision at this level are set out, and examples of the latest version of the diagnostic questionnaire, together with the feedback form that supports the provision of the revised module, conclude the case study.

The information literacy module was introduced in 1998 at the University of North London accompanied by a move towards a student-centred provision through the application of problem-based learning underpinned by innovative uses of ICT. The premise that information literacy is an essential attribute of the successful independent learner was taken as the starting point of this development. In particular, inform-ation literacy was seen as underpinning a student-centred learning environment, in which learners require information-handling skills to interact effectively with a wide range of resources. Students needed to develop these skills to engage successfully with information gathering, manipulation and presentation techniques needed by the discipline-specific curricula. In addition, the implementation of an e-learning strategy in DASS has compounded the need for information literacy skills, as provision is increasingly reliant on web-based resources and virtual learning environments (VLEs). Here students are expected to interact with information coming in a variety of formats and from a range of sources (digital and printed); they therefore need to be information literate:

- to use the information systems effectively, to access and manipulate the information found;

- to filter the irrelevant information (and avoid problems of information overload);

- to present and communicate this information in a way that is appropriate to the task at hand, whether during their academic or professional career.

Information literacy module outline

In line with ALA's definition of information literacy, the module aimed to enhance the academic performance of learners by developing skills that enabled students to locate, manipulate, retrieve, evaluate and present information, including e-mail communication, through effective interaction with customised web resources and ICT facilities available at the University. In addition to the development of basic ICT skills required to access learning materials and general University systems, the syllabus covered searching and evaluative skills needed to retrieve and use the information effectively, together with document-presentation skills, with particular emphasis on referencing and bibliographic competences that were suited to social science disciplines.[2]

Learning outcomes

At the end of the module students should be able to:

1. use essential features of the University's ICT facilities effectively and appropriately;
2. integrate the skills of locating, evaluating, processing and presenting information, using both printed and online formats;
3. develop ICT skills to ECDL standards.

Learning and teaching methods

The module was designed to offer a high level of flexibility in terms of delivery and to encourage students' active participation in the learning process. A diagnostic questionnaire at the start of the module enabled students to assess their learning needs in terms of the assessment requirements. Novice users were guided through a 'slow-track' route with full support, whereas expert users could operate entirely as independent learners by working through some or all of the syllabus as required in order to submit the assignments with a minimum of support. Lectures and hands-on workshops in computer labs constituted the main methods of delivery.[3] Electronic resources were provided for all aspects of the module and are available at *http://www.ilit.org*.[4] Support from tutors was also available in both face-to-face and online modes.

Assessment details

Until 2003/4 the module was assessed by two distinct components, each allocated 50 per cent of the overall weighting.

Component 1: Portfolio of ICT tasks demonstrating file management, word processing, e-mail communication and searching skills to query online resources. As illustrated in Chapter 4, the testing of information literacy competences by the portfolio reflected an assessment method that is commonly found in information literacy education. Lawson's (1999) information literacy programme for first-year students covers similar skills, including the ability to query the online catalogue by searching different fields, construct a simple search using 'and/or' operators in a range of online information systems and use e-mail as a method of communication. A more detailed explanation of the portfolio together with some examples of individual tasks is given below.

The portfolio for component 1 consisted of the following tasks:

A table of contents for the portfolio, which was set within specific editing parameters. This tested students' word-processing and document design competences.

A curriculum vitae (CV) with accompanying letter (as per the guidelines in the panel below). This task encouraged students to develop their reflection on a profile of skills that would be valuable for job-seeking purposes. Feedback from students has shown that this was a very useful task because it helped them improve the content and design of their CV, and therefore enhance their employability.

Guidelines for the CV and accompanying letter

Produce a CV processed to the following template:
Structure: Information should be organised in the following order:

1. Personal details (name, address, date of birth).
2. Educational history and qualifications, listed in reverse chronological order.
3. Work experience, in reverse chronological order; interests, achievements (no more than two pages in length).

Editing: Tabs, tables, or indents should be used to display the dated information. Base font should be 11 point Times New Roman or Arial. Headings should be bold, main headings bold and 14 point. Margins, line spacing, and spacing between paragraphs are a matter for your judgment. Check your text for spelling, punctuation, and consistent use of spacing and text style.

Covering letter: Produce a simple letter submitting the CV in application for the post of xxx to xxxx (employer name and address). You must explain why you want the job and what you can offer if appointed. Make sure the name, address and text style of the letter match that of the CV.

A range of searching activities covering the use of the online library catalogue and the newspaper database. These tasks introduced students to the online facilities in some cases for the first time, and were therefore an essential induction to searching and evaluating skills, as students were required to access the information and interact with it in order to answer a series of set questions. Guidelines for this are detailed below.

Using the University's OPAC catalogue

Answer the questions listed below for the following reference: Scott, J. The old boy network in Giddens A (ed) (2001) *Sociology Introductory Readings*:

1. How many copies of this book are available for loan in total?
2. What is the shelfmark for this book?
3. How many counterloan copies are in the library?
4. What is the name of the module which contains this item in its reading list?

Finding information using the online newspaper database

Access the required articles to answer the following:

In January 2004 an interview with a silversmithing graduate of London Metropolitan University was published. When she was looking for the course, why did the one at this University keep coming up as recommended?

These are illustrative examples of tasks using the OPAC and the newspaper database.

Evidence of e-mail communication with one of the module tutors (see guidelines, below).

Guidelines on the e-mail correspondence with the tutor

Identify and outline a topic of your choice and send this to the module's tutor. Print out the e-mail correspondence that contains your original e-mail and the tutor's reply approving the topic you have chosen to research. You can use Webmail or any other e-mail software.

In the subject box type the module code and a brief description of the content of the e-mail, e.g. *Topic selected for Component 2*

In the message include: your surname, initial and ID number.

Attach a Microsoft Word document that briefly outlines the aspect of the topic you wish to tackle. You need to be specific and narrow the focus of your topic.

This activity was developed for two specific purposes:

- To familiarise students with e-mail communication facilities. Comments from the self-reflection reports showed that initially students were often not competent in sending attachments even when they were active e-mail users. However, as suggested by the feedback, students soon discovered the time-saving benefit provided by the use of attachments, which they then used to e-mail draft assignments and general documentation supporting assessment-related queries to tutors.

- To provide formative feedback on the students' choice of topic and on their attempts to formulate a search strategy.

E-mail support has also generated the unforeseen benefit of providing feedback outside of the sessions timetabled by the module, and of offering practice in written communication. Students who were very weak in this area were easily identified through the completion of this task and extra support in written communication skills was made available to tackle this problem. Examples of poor e-mail correspondence, such as those shown below, were made available to students to illustrate the problem of formulating a topic that has too wide a focus and is poorly explained.

Example 1

The topic that I have chosen is related to the history of advertising. I will look at all the information regarding advertising in the nineteenth century. In advertising, media refers to the means of communication, such as television, radio, books and newspapers. By looking at the distinct aspect at this specific period, it will become easier to answers questions such as: what is advertising, why does advertising become relevant to the media, what kinds of bodies were interested in it, how advertising was affecting society, how advertising agencies were targeting the public? Starting at those points, I will be able to make some contrasts and to analyse the effects of it. It encompasses all the different issues that have allowed advertisers to come up with some good and bad effects. However, at the end I should be able to understand the major impacts that the media has had on society.

Example 2

I am writing to you for the second assessment of the information literacy module. The topic that I would like to research is: the impact of reality shows on human privacy.

A self-evaluation report requiring students to reflect on their experience of developing information literacy skills (see guidelines, below). The tutor's reflections on the impact of this task are articulated under the section on the 2001/2 – survey of students' feedback covering the example of diagnostic and post-testing. The detailed evaluation of what students have learned is presented in a later section on the students' reflection on the module to illustrate the overall impact of information literacy provision at this level.

Guidelines for the self-evaluation report

In this activity students are required to reflect on their learning experience of information literacy by addressing the following questions in a 500-word report.

1. What did you learn in the information literacy module?

2. Were the learning resources useful in developing your searching skills? (Use one of the following systems used in this module to illustrate your example: online newspaper database, online catalogue or Google.)

3. Were the learning resources useful in developing your evaluative skills? (Use one of the following tutorials used in this module to illustrate your example: Internet Detective, basic Google search.)

4. Which areas covered by the module did you find easiest and which most difficult? (ICT, searching for and evaluating information.)

5. How do you expect to use your information literacy skills in your future studies?

Component 2: Small research project demonstrating searching and evaluative skills using a search engine (see guidelines overleaf). The small research project consisted of a search strategy for a topic of the student's choice using Google.[5] Students here were required to formulate an appropriate search and to evaluate the first 10 sites retrieved according to specific criteria, including relevance, reliability, currency and authority of the source. The selection of these criteria was based on similar practice presented in the literature (Oberman et al., 1988; Grafstein, 2002) as well as the examples taken from the Internet Detective tutorial.[6] Carlson and Repman argue that teaching first-year students to use the Web effectively is essential because the Web is often the first, and sometimes the only, information resource students will use. In their experience, web-searching skills are 'a critical building block of information literacy' (Carlson and Repman, 2002: 22), as students are not effective web searchers from the outset.

Assessment guidelines for the small research project

Complete a search using Google (NB use *http://www.google.co.uk*). You can search any topic you like as long as it is approved by a module tutor. The written evaluation you submit should have a maximum length of 1500 words and should contain information on the following:

Formulation and construction of the search

This section should contain:

A brief description of the topic researched, i.e. what angle are you adopting? (See the guidelines and examples on the formulation and construction of a search under Component 2 of the information literacy DASS option, *http://www.ilit.org*.)

Detailed explanation of the search strategy used to find relevant information on this topic. This should include a rationale supporting your keyword selection and search strategy method used. Remember you need to describe only one search strategy and the set of results (i.e. first 10 websites) found by this strategy. (Do not write an essay on the topic.)

Evaluation of the information found

This section should give a detailed evaluation of the success of your search strategy by assessing the quality of the information contained in the first 10 websites retrieved. Remember you need to provide detailed evaluation for each of the first 10 sites found (see tutorial on criteria for evaluation, on the webpage). A Google printout of the list of these results should be added as Appendix 1 to illustrate evidence of the search.

Assessment criteria

To pass this assessment you must:

- Clearly identify the topic you are researching.
- Have formulated and constructed one search strategy, e.g. Boolean operators, phrase searching; these strategies may be used in combination. Single keyword searching is not sufficient and will result in a fail.
- Give detailed evaluation of the search used and the quality of the information found in the first 10 websites.
- Include as Appendix 1 the list of first 10 websites retrieved.
- Word-process your report, paying attention to clarity of expression, grammar, spelling and punctuation.

Information literacy and instructional design

Mellon (1988) argues that it is important to pitch information literacy provision at the right level of complexity so that first-year undergraduate students develop threshold-level information-handling and evaluative skills required for academic work. The approach proposed by Mellon takes into account the fact that the majority of these students do not possess the cognitive abilities to adopt open-ended strategies dictated by the online environment, where there is no right or wrong answer, and where the outcome is dependent on the use of sophisticated critical and evaluative skills. This point is supported by the findings of a study on the information literacy module for social science at the University, where students were unable to define the focus of a research topic, identify appropriate terminology and apply effective search strategies (Andretta, 2002). To address this problem, information literacy provision within the department is based on the principles of reiteration and progression, characterised by the structuring of learning resources in a step-by-step fashion and reinforced by numerous exercises. A study by Kuhlthau (1988) has shown that students find this approach easy to follow and therefore are encouraged to use the learning resources for a range of applications. The following comment from a student who attended the information literacy module seems to confirm this view:

> The handbook illustrated different search techniques, e.g. phrase searching [...] hopefully I can apply [these] to future projects. I [shall] keep the booklets from this module and go through them again, but this time trying to search for different information.[7]

Furthermore, the learning resources were supported by a plethora of visual clues to enable students to check their progress and orientate their learning. Practice on instructional design developed to support this module has shown that visual information, complementing the step-by-step approach, worked very well, and these combined methods were particularly effective when used to illustrate activities involving the interaction with a computer, such as querying the online library catalogue or using a search engine on the Web. This approach also encouraged learning through active participation, as advocated by De Ruiter (2002: 199): 'Instructions should be hands-on; demonstration is far less effective'. This is because the speed of the demonstration is too fast for the learner to follow, whereas instructional material gives the learner control over the pace at which the learning takes place. However, practice in DASS has shown that the most effective way to employ instructional resources is to complement their use with an initial demonstration on how to access these. De Ruiter also comments that:

> Every action must be described in detail to make sure that a procedure can be executed correctly. Apart from this, it is important to describe the results of any action [...] to enable the user to check whether he or she is still on the right course. (Ibid.: 202)

This method was used to structure the learning resources of the information literacy module, and an example of the step-by-step approach is illustrated by the guidelines on the formulation of the search process. According to Grafstein, students need to engage with the full searching process, which involves the initial 'breaking down of a topic from discursive formulation into keywords' (Grafstein, 2002: 201). In the small research project students were exposed to the complete process of search formulation and construction starting with the need to translate a general topic of interest into a focused topic of research. Practice has shown that most students are not familiar with this process and find the breaking down of a topic extremely difficult (Kuhlthau, 1988; Andretta, 2002). Initially the search formulation process was disseminated in a handbook that covered the full searching process. Exercises were placed at the end of each section to consolidate the learning process and to ensure that students mastered all the stages required to formulate an effective searching strategy. However, feedback demonstrated that the students found the format of these instructions rather unfriendly as the searching process and the supporting learning activities were described as difficult to understand and to follow. Observation of students during lab-based activities confirmed that there was a need to break down the searching process into smaller tasks so that clear prompts could guide a novice learner through the stages of such a complex strategy. To address this problem a step-by-step tutorial was introduced to demonstrate the stages involved in developing a basic search using Google. The tutorial is shown below and is divided into two parts: the search formulation and the search construction. The example used in this tutorial is based on a search performed by a student with explanations of each stage added by the tutor to guide the learner through the searching process.

Example of a basic search formulation for Google

1. Identify the topic you wish to research
Let us suppose you wish to find research procedures for people wanting to adopt children from abroad. This topic is too wide and needs narrowing down by addressing the following questions: Which procedures? e.g. legal procedures Which particular group of people? e.g. British parents What country are the children from? e.g. China
2. Narrow the topic down to a specific focus
The focus of the topic therefore becomes: Chinese legal procedure for British parents intending to adopt a child
3. Formulate a search strategy using Google
Using the topic of Chinese legal procedure for British parents intending to adopt a child
a. Do a preliminary search.
Type the main terms from this topic into the subject box of Google: Chinese legal procedure British parents adoption *Note* that some of the words contained in the original topic have been omitted or changed. The formulation of the search strategy starts here by: Omitting stop words [for, the] Using nouns to describe the topic [adoption instead of adopting]
b. Look at the first 10 sites found by the preliminary search and answer the following questions for each site examined: What angle of the topic is this site covering? Is this the angle I want to adopt for my search? If *yes* then you need to look at the keywords the site uses to describe the topic and decide whether these are more suitable than the ones you have used in your initial search If *no* then move on to the next site until you find the one covering the topic that interests you Once you have found the angle you want to research, ask yourself the following questions:
■ Do you want to change any of the original keywords?
Make a note of the terms you have changed and why; this will become useful when you complete Component 2

- Do you want to change any of the order of display of the keywords?

For example, what would happen if I changed the order of the keywords in the following query?

(Complete the search in Google including these amendments to answer these questions.)

Chinese legal procedure British parents adoption
British parents adoption Chinese legal procedure

4. Construction of the search

Now that you have selected your keywords you need to find the best way to combine these terms into a search

Boolean operators

Use the Boolean *AND* to link the keywords together:

Chinese AND legal AND procedure AND British AND parents AND adoption

Google however uses AND by default so we can omit this. The search therefore would become:

Chinese legal procedure adoption British parents

Use the Boolean *OR* to expand your search:

Parents OR parent would retrieve sites that contain either term so increase your chance of finding relevant information.

So your Boolean search strategy would look like this:

Chinese legal procedure adoption British parents OR parent

Phrase searching

We can now implement the phrase searching strategy to narrow the focus of the search:

"Chinese legal adoption procedure" British parents OR parent

The final search strategy would therefore consist of:

Boolean AND by default

Boolean OR to find sites containing parent as well as parents

Phrase search to find sites that contain the phrase enclosed in " " (quotation marks)

5. Preliminary evaluation of the sites found

Look at the first 10 sites and answer the following questions:

- How many sites has Google retrieved in total? (This will give you a rough indication of how effective your search is.)
- Are the results relevant to the topic you are researching?
- For a detailed tutorial on how to evaluate web-based information complete the Internet Detective tutorial on the ilit.org website.

This tutorial was introduced in 2003/4 in response to the problems encountered by previous cohorts when attempting to develop a search strategy for the small research project. Comparison between the cohorts of 2002/3 and 2003/4 revealed that students' comments from the self-evaluation task in 2003/4, after this basic search tutorial was introduced, displayed greater awareness of the search process. This was reflected in the use of the terminology associated with searching activities, such as the elimination of stop-list words or the application of a phrase search strategy, as well as acknowledgments on the importance and usefulness of narrowing the scope of the topic in preparation for a search. By contrast, students' self-evaluation reports in 2002/3 showed a distinct lack of familiarity with the terminology and did not include any comments on the benefit of effective searching strategies. This suggests that the step-by-step approach was successful in helping students to master complex searching skills at this basic level of provision.

The plug-and-play structure

The module was developed taking into account the basic premise promoted by Repman and Carlson, who acknowledge that, given the large number of students and the wide-ranging levels of experience and abilities that characterise the student body, the information literacy programme must adopt a flexible delivery and must be individually tailored. Their solution is to produce an accurate profile of students, in terms of both skills and affective attitude, and to address their learning needs at an individual level:

> We provide our students with this information literacy framework and foundation through in-class lecture and demonstration. Even more important is how we follow through by providing distributed, targeted, hands-on practice. These two exercises have worked well for us and can be adapted to almost any kind of HE setting ... We encourage students to use assignments from any of their classes for this activity. Students have to describe strategies used and evaluate their results in terms of the usefulness of the information retrieved. (Repman and Carlson, 2002: 25)

Booth and Fabian also comment that effective information literacy instruction must be based on the following principles: 'context specificity, usefulness to learner, multiple opportunities for learning, rapid feedback, availability of remediation, incremental instruction, transferable skills and modular design' (Booth and Fabian, 2002: 126). In line with these perspectives a 'plug-and-play' structure (Andretta and Cutting, 2003: 204) was devised to offer flexibility of provision within a multidisciplinary environment and, at the same time, to address the learning needs of an increasingly diverse body of students. In the context of the information literacy module the plug-and-play method[8] operated as follows:

- Students completed a web-based diagnostic questionnaire where they rated their information literacy skills according to three distinct levels of competence: novice, intermediate and advanced in the three main areas covered by the module, namely ICT, searching and evaluating skills.

- The feedback generated by the questionnaire produced an individualised learning profile that, when used in conjunction with the general assessment timetable, helped students to pace their progress through the assessed portfolio.

Students were therefore encouraged to take responsibility for their learning by first assessing their initial level of information literacy competences, and consequently, by working through the interactive web-based tutorials devised to address the weaknesses raised by their learning profile, to complete the assessment tasks successfully. Plug-and-play in this context implied that there was no single route to the learning process; on the contrary, interaction with the tutorials was determined by the learning profile generated by the diagnostic questionnaire, so that for example if a student scored highly in ICT skills, but was a novice in searching and evaluative skills, then he/she could skip the ICT practice and concentrate on tutorials that focus on searching and evaluative competences.

Examples of diagnostic and post-testing

During the course of this module the methods of pre- and post-diagnostic testing have changed substantially as the module has evolved in response to the students' needs and institutionally-driven initiatives. The first restructuring of the diagnostic testing occurred at the end of the pilot in the academic year 2000/1, the second editing was undertaken in

2001/2 and the most recent one was in May 2004. The editing in these cases altered the questionnaire radically in terms of structure, content and method of survey. An outline of these changes illustrates their impact on the flexibility of delivery, and on the students' level of engagement. These instances are examined under two headings: diagnostic questionnaire, referring to the pre-test method, and the survey of students' feedback associated with the post-test approach.

2000/1 – diagnostic questionnaire

The diagnostic questionnaire was distributed at the beginning of the module with the aim of generating profiles of the students' information literacy skills. This survey comprised an initial explanation of the purpose of the questionnaire followed by five main parts, including an introductory section on personal details used as the basis for statistical analysis of general issues such as gender, age and access to computer equipment. The remaining four sections covered basic ICT skills, Internet use and competences in searching and evaluating information from the Web within the general subject area of information ethics, and exploring the impact of technology on the information society. There were several problems with this first version of the questionnaire:

- At a logistical level the questionnaire was disseminated in printed format and calculation of the scores had to be performed manually for all the four information literacy sections. Not surprisingly this process was extremely cumbersome when applied to a large cohort of 150 students. In addition, students did not feel a sense of ownership of the diagnostic process as evaluation of their information literacy skills was undertaken by the tutor.
- At a learner level the majority of the students scored highly in the ICT section and automatically assumed that competence in this area would be sufficient to pass the module.

2000/1 – survey of students' feedback

An attitude questionnaire was distributed at the end of the pilot to assess the students' perception of any improvement of their information literacy skills, as well as to gather feedback on the effectiveness of the learning resources and the quality of delivery. This survey remained anonymous to ensure that students did not feel inhibited when providing their assessment of the module, and therefore the personal details section was limited to identifying gender and mode of study. Other sections focused on the effectiveness of specific electronic and printed learning resources on the students' assessment of their level of IT literacy and their searching and evaluative skills before and after the module. The questionnaire showed that despite exhibiting low information literacy skills on entry, students 'claimed considerable improvements in all skills associated with IL on completion of the module' (Andretta, 2001: 262). This type of spontaneous feedback process, however, generated a very low response, which made the results unrepresentative, raising questions regarding the reliability of the data. For example, out of a cohort of 150 students, only 27 completed the attitude questionnaire giving a return rate of 18 per cent, which is too low to be statistically significant or to support any sound conclusion.

Extracts from the results from this survey shown in the tables below illustrated that students registered an improvement in all the skills covered by the module, although a greater degree of improvement was perceived in the areas of ICT and evaluative skills. What is missing from this survey method is the qualitative data that would enable a contextualisation of the students' perceived improvement of their information literacy skills.

Extracts from the results of the attitude survey[9]

Q14. How would you rate your ICT skills?

	Good	Average	Poor	Don't know
Before starting this module (%)	11	37	48	4
After completing this module (%)	44	48	4	4

Q15. How would you rate your searching skills using online resources?

	Good	Average	Poor	Don't know
Before starting this module (%)	12	38	50	0
After completing this module (%)	52	48	0	0

Q16. How would you rate your evaluation skills in relation to the information found?

	Good	Average	Poor	Don't know
Before starting this module (%)	11	37	48	4
After completing this module (%)	35	54	0	12

The over-reliance on quantitative data to measure the impact of the module was deemed unsuitable to evaluate the less tangible effects of transferability of skills and increased level of independent learning. As a result, an alternative method of fostering students' self-evaluation was sought and this is discussed in detail under the 2001/2 section.

A question on attendance at the module was asked at the end of this survey to ascertain the impact of the plug-and-play approach and the adoption of voluntary attendance. Compulsory attendance was perceived as going against the principles of independent learning and of flexible delivery that the module aimed to achieve and was therefore rejected from the outset. However, it was decided to explore the students' reaction to voluntary attendance given the 'spoon-feeding' expectations they had expressed during the module, which had caused some difficulties when interacting with the learning resources. Twelve out of the 27 students in the sample claimed that their learning would have improved had attendance been compulsory.[10] When asked to elaborate on their answer the students in this category saw compulsory attendance as a positive influence on their learning, as this comment suggests: 'I would have attended all the classes and [would] have been up-to-date. At the moment I am lagging behind'.[11]

2001/2 – diagnostic questionnaire

In 2001/2, a web-based version of the questionnaire was introduced and the scoring, as well as the generation of the students' overall profile, became fully automated. This meant that students could claim ownership of the whole diagnostic process as they had direct access to the feedback form identifying their level of competences. The form could also be saved and consulted by the students to help them plan a customised programme of study that suited their learning needs.

The skills tested by the questionnaire were categorised under the three main areas of the syllabus:

- A basic *ICT skills* section assessing the students' competence in activities such as file management, windows manipulation, electronic communication and word-processing, together with elementary Internet skills such as navigation and use of search engines.

- A *searching skills* section testing the students' knowledge of searching strategies required to interact with a range of online systems.

- An *evaluation skills* section assessing their awareness of the evaluation criteria required to assess information in terms of currency, relevance and reliability.

The original information literacy syllabus contained a section on information ethics; this was dropped during the 2001/2 academic year because it became clear that the subject of information ethics was too wide and complex to expect an appropriate coverage of this in addition to covering areas of searching and evaluating practices. Information ethics had provided the focus of the second assignment, consisting of a Google-based search task and by dropping this part of the syllabus students were encouraged to select their own topic of research. This gave them the opportunity to transfer their information literacy skills as they began to look for information required to complete other assignments. Comments from the self-evaluation reports illustrated that such a move further emphasised the usefulness of the information literacy competences developed by this module and increased students' motivation to develop these skills. Practice elsewhere (Creanor and Durnell, 1994; Lawson, 1999) also supports the findings that students' motivation is linked to the contextualisation of the information literacy skills in the subjects studied. In addition, dropping information ethics from the syllabus gave more time to develop the searching and evaluation skills sections by increasing the number of online resources tested by the portfolio. As a result, academic sources such as the online catalogue and the newspaper database were introduced to complement the Google-based search. Content analysis of the self-evaluation report, examined later, shows that mature students were particularly vulnerable here because of the lack of familiarity with these facilities, which precluded any independent interaction with them. Similar conclusions are presented by the work of Branch and Gilchrist, who identify factors that inhibit access to information resources, such as 'reading level, fear, English as a second language, as well as non-traditional background of learners' (Branch and Gilchrist, 1996: 478).

A more elaborate explanation of the diagnostic questionnaire and the types of competences it assessed was also introduced at this time to eliminate any misunderstanding on the part of the students that intermediate or advanced ICT skills would make them information literate. This strategy has been successful in raising students' awareness of information literacy beyond ICT competences, and this is shown by comparing the content of the students' feedback generated in 2000/1 and 2001/2. In the former, students commented favourably about overcoming their 'fear of computers', whereas in the latter the feedback provided a more comprehensive picture of the set of skills developed during the module. These included not only ICT, but also searching for and evaluating information, interacting with online information systems and improving design skills to enhance word-processed documents like the CV.

2001/2 – survey of students' feedback

We were keen to evaluate the level of transferability of the skills developed during the module, and the need to rethink the students' self-evaluation process gave the opportunity to do so from the students' perspective. The voluntary feedback was replaced by a self-assessment task inviting students to reflect on their learning. When this assessment was run for the first time, students were asked to address a series of questions but were not compelled to use them to structure their report in a question-and-answer format. As a result the quality of the feedback showed a lack of structure and a limited level of self-analysis. Once the students were asked to use the questions to structure their self-evaluation report, however, there were considerable improvements in the students' use of examples to illustrate a point, in the quality of self-reflection and in the level of confidence they developed in their independent learning abilities. Posting examples of good and bad self-evaluations on the website, produced by previous cohorts, also helped the students become aware of what the self-evaluative process entailed and promoted better understanding of how to tackle this task. Finally, making the self-reflective exercise part of the assessment ensured a high return rate of the students' feedback on their learning experience. The highly representative feedback has also provided an effective input into the quality assurance of the module, directing the restructuring of provision and the editing of the learning resources in a never-ending cycle of practice and reflection.

Students' reflection on the information literacy module: what have you learned?

This section is based on the analysis of the students' self-evaluation reports from the provision of the information literacy module spanning the academic years of 2001/2, 2002/3 and 2003/4. A phenomenographic approach was used in accordance with information literacy practice by

Bruce (1997) and Lupton (2004) as this model suits the reflective and qualitative nature of the data generated by the self-evaluation exercise. Lupton's description of this type of data analysis reflects the approach used to derive meaning from the students' feedback. She defines the phenomenographic approach as involving the:

> Use of an iterative process where there is a search for meaning (how the phenomenon is experienced) and structure (the relationship between different ways of experiencing). The iteration takes [the] form of reading the transcripts and search for similarities and differences in ways of experiencing the phenomenon. (Lupton, 2004: 47)

The findings were structured into main themes generated by the comments on the type of skills students had developed or improved, their feedback on the usefulness of specific resources and examples of transferability of information skills acquired as a result of the module. When asked to reflect on the extent of their learning, the students identified two main categories: ICT and information literacy skills. The former was described using a range of terms, including IT, ICT computer literacy and computer usage. Information literacy skills, by contrast, were identified and quantified by listing the types of activities covered by the module, such as searching a number of information systems and evaluating the information found on the Internet.

ICT skills

When referring to ICT, students commented that this part of the module was very practical and useful particularly in relation to enhancing the design and presentation of word-processed documents: 'Improved skills related to computer usage – especially [the] formatting of documents. My CV and accompanying letter now have a professional look'. Other comments reflected a wide spectrum of competences in ICT, which ranged from complete novice to users with some ICT skills. The former was illustrated by the following comment:

> I have learned a lot from the information literacy module, such as being able to use e-mail to send and receive messages and download attachments; how to format a disk, which I had no idea

about before I came on the course; how to download information from one drive to another; and downloading information from the Internet.

Effective document design skills was seen as enhancing existing ICT competences:

> Although I had some IT skills before starting this module I was not very confident with them. At the end of the module, I have improved the IT skills that I had and have gained some new ones. This has made me more confident in the use of computers. For example, I have learned more complex word-processing skills such as inserting a header/footer into a document; [and] I can now use the University's e-mail system.

Students with advanced ICT skills also provided an interesting insight regarding the initial assumptions they made about the information literacy module and in the type of skills they lacked despite their competence in computer usage.

> As I have reasonable computer skills I thought that this module would not teach me anything new. Instead I found the module interesting because it opened up to me things that I didn't know about [like] searching the Internet.

Poor searching skills when interacting with the Internet were identified by most students in this category, and in this respect the module addressed a fundamental information literacy requirement by fostering competences in the formulation and construction stages of the search process:

> I am very familiar with computers; however, the information literacy module has definitely opened my eyes to searching for information on the Internet. Now I can construct far more specific and sophisticated search strategies and get better results.

Even those students who claimed long-term use of computers found that the information literacy module enhanced their competence in accessing information:

Although I have 20 years of work experience in IT this module has improved my searching skills using Google and the newspaper database.

One student, whose work relies heavily on information-seeking activities, still found the module relevant:

Having been a computer engineer in the past and currently being a Parliamentary Research and Information Officer for a major UK charity, conducting Internet-based research, managing information and presenting it for public consumption is central to my job. [Information literacy] did not particularly enhance my information skills; nonetheless, the assessment did give me the opportunity to brush up on some of the basics.[12]

Information literacy skills

The unique nature of information literacy was reflected in the comments from a student who did not know what the module entailed:

When I first started the information literacy module I wasn't sure what to expect. I thought it may provide a guide to using a computer, but it was actually a far more rewarding experience. This module taught me the basic skills used to research and evaluate information and the most effective way to do this.

Feedback on the overall impact of the module was reassuringly positive as students seemed to appreciate the opportunity to develop skills in areas with which most of them were either unfamiliar or in which they did not feel competent. Effective interaction with a range of sources was often rated as the most useful competence this module had helped them to develop because of its application to other areas of the degree:

The most important thing I have learned from this module was my ability to further my knowledge in the use of information resources that are vital to my politics degree. I was able to use the online library catalogue for the first time, something I didn't imagine was possible.

Not surprisingly students with poor information literacy skills on entry commented favourably on the substantial amount of knowledge acquired as a result of this module:

> I had little knowledge of the Internet. After a few weeks [of the module] I have learned so much and can create a more specific search to find information for my politics and philosophy assignment. My searching, evaluating and formatting skills have also improved.

Even when students had some experience of the Internet they were able to enhance their searching skills:

> [I] gained a lot of knowledge from the information literacy module on how to complete a simple Internet search. I had carried out Internet searches before, but as a result of this module, I have learned to make more effective use of a search engine.

Specific aspects of searching were identified as particularly useful, such as narrowing the search by using appropriate keywords or by employing specific field searching strategies, like author, title or year of publication. These techniques were applied across the range of the sources available:

> This proved to be of great benefit for later tasks as it enabled me to take note of all the tools available to conduct and narrow a search, whether on the Internet, using the newspaper database or even the University library catalogue.

Similarly, the module made students aware of the importance of evaluating information to ensure that the source was reliable:

> My evaluation skills have improved because of this module. Asking who wrote what, how often a website is updated and which organisation is responsible for the site are important questions that need to be investigated when retrieving information from the Internet.

Searching and evaluating techniques were also perceived as valuable in the general manipulation of information:

The information literacy module has given me more in-depth knowledge about processing information. Improvements in my searching and evaluating techniques have enabled me to use the information more carefully.

Feedback on specific resources covered by the module

Online newspaper database

The majority of students were ignorant of the online newspaper database before attending the information literacy module and this is clearly reflected in the following comment often made by students who reflected on this resource: 'I had no idea it existed before taking this module'. Owing to this lack of familiarity, becoming acquainted with this database was perceived as challenging and generated negative expectations based on previous unsuccessful attempts to interact with this resource: 'Being a first-time user of the database I assumed that locating the information I needed would be difficult. This assumption rested on previous experience where searches generated hundreds of results'.[13]

Once this resource became familiar it was seen as: 'an extremely useful', 'a valuable' and 'a really helpful' source for articles that would improve students' quality of research and help them to find information relevant to other assignments: '[the newspaper database] helped me find an article for an assignment on poverty and social exclusion'. Similarly, another comment illustrated the positive experience of a student engaging for the first time with this resource: 'At the beginning this was very unfamiliar. It soon became one of my favourite databases and was especially useful for my research into the history of the press'.

Online library catalogue

Although this resource was unfamiliar to some students, feedback did not express the same level of ignorance about the library catalogue compared with that given for the online newspaper database. The comments here indicated that in this case unfamiliarity was not caused by students' lack of knowledge of the system, but by their inability to use it. As a result, students developed unfounded negative expectations about the system: '[before I undertook this module] I had never used this service and had never attempted to use it as I expected it to be very difficult'. However, as soon as the hurdle of unfamiliarity was overcome, the positive aspects of using the catalogue were realised: 'before this module I didn't know how to use the catalogue; after two weeks of this module I was able to access the online catalogue, check books and renew my loans'. Similarly, another student admitted that:

> [This module is] exceptionally useful. [Prior to it] I did not know how to find books and often ended up with the wrong book or author. This ate into my study time. Now I can find the author, the publisher, year of publication, where the book is [located] and how many copies are available.

Learning how to use the library catalogue was therefore seen as offering a number of benefits by all the students. Enhanced and faster access to the stock were often quoted as examples of these benefits: '[the catalogue ...] made searching for books much easier than having to go through each shelf manually'. Different searching features were mentioned by students in describing how to decipher the classification system: 'the online catalogue has made borrowing books easier because once I have found the classmark I can easily locate the book on the shelf'. Another example included the correct interpretation of the bibliographic rules associated with edited books and different types of authors: 'after much practice I have learned how to make an Author/Title search and can find edited books as well as corporate authors'.[14]

The library catalogue exercise, as with the tasks on the newspaper database, was also appreciated for the transferable skills it provided. Once the students developed the searching skills to query the catalogue correctly, its use expanded to address the requirements of other modules: '[it] gave me the opportunity to search the availability and location of certain key texts needed for another module'. The library catalogue and newspaper database were placed at the same level in terms of transferability and usefulness:

> [The module was] very beneficial as I became familiar with the library and newspaper online catalogues. I found this priceless as it certainly helped me to research for books and journal articles for other assignments. Task 3 [the online catalogue exercise] helped me complete a bibliography needed for an essay.

Google

Students' feedback on the Google exercise illustrated that the development of Internet searching skills was extremely useful in addressing the problem of information overload: '[before this module] I had used Google but I never used "and", "or" and "not" commands. Now that I have used them I see how these commands help in filtering information'. As with the learning experience generated by the other two resources, students described their skills in this area as poor prior to the module: 'before I undertook [information literacy] I was unaware of how to formulate and construct a search [using] search techniques such as Boolean, phrase searching, stop words and + sign, so my searches were of poor quality'. Additionally, a lack of searching skills had meant that much time was spent looking for information, which usually was not relevant to the topic researched:

> Previously it was very much a matter of hit and miss. I have always found it time-consuming typing any word that seemed close to the subject [I needed to research], but all I would get would be irrelevant information. In this module I have learned about using Boolean search techniques [to] eliminate irrelevant information.

Similarly, another student acknowledged that the module has shortened the time spent looking for information: '[it] greatly assisted me with [finding] relevant information that would previously have required a number of trials to obtain'.

Students acknowledged the importance of narrowing the scope of the search through the processes of search formulation and construction to produce relevant results: 'Before I often used wide-ranging topics to search for subjects on the Internet and never got the information I needed. [The searching techniques I have learned are therefore] time saving'. The next comment is particularly significant because students at this level have difficulties in identifying terms that best describe their topics and, at the same time, limit the parameters of the search: '[It was] useful because it taught me how to narrow down the scope of my search through the use of keywords'.

Future use of information literacy skills

When asked whether they would use the information literacy skills developed in this module, all the students identified the relevance of these competences in supporting their future academic career: 'I feel I now have the skills to help me to research any subject effectively and with ease, and so I will be putting my new skills into practice throughout my future studies with projects, coursework and revision'.

In addition, the transferability of information literacy skills was illustrated through the use of these competences to tackle academic tasks outside the module. For example, searching and bibliographic skills were applied to find sources relevant to their degree as a whole:

> [This was] useful because I can apply skills learned in this module to my other modules; [for example] the literature search required for the assessment helped me to search for books I needed for my course.

Other instances of transferability involved a more effective interaction with all the information sources available from the increased use of appropriate Internet sources for essays, to a greater reliance on the online database to access articles (although, judging by how this was commented upon, the use of such a resource may have been extended to the personal need to remain informed of current news):

> I will be more inclined to incorporate information found on the Web into research for essay topics as I have gained the skills to filter through sites and recognise reputable ones. Previously I have relied heavily on textbooks for information but this can now change. I am also pleased that I can search for newspaper articles online as I do not read newspapers religiously and can now find articles that I would have otherwise missed.

Students also identified specific modules in which information literacy skills had been particularly relevant: 'through the use of Google, searching techniques and the newspaper database I was able to get relevant information on an essay I was writing on the European Union and the United States'. Others commented on the expanded research opportunities that have become available thanks to the information literacy skills they have developed: 'A valuable asset pointing me in the right direction for further research now I can use the online resources of the British library'.

One of the most substantial benefits was the increased confidence that students claimed to have developed in accomplishing information literacy tasks:

> The module will not only help in my future studies but throughout life [it] will also enable me to use my time effectively and with other components of my degree. I now feel confident to go on the Net and produce a substantial search and evaluation.

This seems to have had an empowering effect on their academic performance and a diminishing effect on the level of frustration experienced when trying to access information through less effective and therefore slower methods:

> [The development of] searching and evaluative skills helped me feel far more confident and in control of structuring research for my coursework at the University. Also, I no longer feel frustrated when trying to obtain original journals as this previously took a long time; now I can browse and download articles from these journals online.

These effects are in line with Carr's view of self-directed learning, which is 'concerned much more with an internal change of consciousness than with the external management of instructional events' (Carr, 1986: 335). The increased confidence in information-seeking activities was also seen as fundamental for academic life:

> What I have learned from this module will be used as a good basis throughout my university degree. I feel a lot more confident about finding information on the Internet and [the facilities at] the University.

Another benefit that was often commented on by the students was the amount of time saved thanks to the information literacy skills developed. These included not just a quicker but also a more effective interaction with all the information systems encountered during the module:

> [The information literacy skills] will help me to find and evaluate information on the Internet, which is needed for most of my research projects. It will save me time; for example I can check the OPAC to reserve books and ensure that travelling to the university will not be a waste of time.

Time saving was also associated with newly acquired e-mailing skills as students became aware of the usefulness of this medium in keeping in touch with their tutors without having to travel to the University: 'It is great being able to send lecturers a copy of a drafted piece of work, and so [I can] cut down on my travelling time to and from the University'. Similarly, another student commented on the usefulness of e-mail communication in replacing the personal delivery of draft coursework: 'now that I am aware of how to send e-mail attachments, I will e-mail drafts of assignments rather than running around the University to find the offices [of the relevant tutors]'.

The impact of the information literacy module can be summarised by two comments that revealed two distinct but complementary aspects of information literacy education and its link to the process of lifelong learning. The first comment offered an insight into the problem-solving nature of the module: 'I gained a better understanding of how to tackle a problem'. The second example illustrated lifelong learning in practice:

> I feel that this module has been very beneficial to me. It has given me an insight into how to improve and better myself. [These skills] will be very handy with the production of coursework. It has truly improved my chances of obtaining a degree.

Some students also commented on how the information literacy skills would enhance their opportunities for employment and for professional development.

> I think that these skills will be useful throughout my university life, but should also help me make the transition from a very practical career (nursing), where my computer skills were poor, to perhaps a more office-based career where these skills are very important.

ICT skills were identified as improving students' employability because of the high demand for these competences by employers:

> The information literacy module is a bonus because it increased my knowledge in ICT. This gives me great confidence in applying my ICT skills to further my studies and to gain employment.

Not surprisingly, the task requiring students to develop their own CV was welcomed because of its use in job-seeking: '[I was able to] update and improve my CV, which will prove a great help in the future when I apply for jobs'. The following comment, however, acknowledges that provision of information literacy covers only the certificate level of the undergraduate programme:[15]

> I know that [my] information literacy skills will be very useful for my studies. As my subject knowledge expands I will probably need news skills in information literacy. It is not possible to become information literate within a few months. But I believe I will go on developing my literacy skills throughout my degree [and] at work.

Feedback from another student illustrated that there was a need to integrate information literacy education at all levels of the degree to prepare learners for more complex research activities:

> My information literacy skills will be ultimately tested when I need to research for future presentations and written work, particularly [when I will be undertaking] a final year dissertation that will require a variety of different sources to be used, for example websites, books and newspaper articles.

Future developments of the information literacy module 2004/5 academic year

From 2004 the independent learning element of the information literacy module will integrate areas of academic literacy, such as essay writing and note-taking,[16] with the problem-solving and evaluative skills required to complete a range of information-related academic tasks. The learning-how-to-learn approach will be based on the development of essential evaluative skills through the diagnostic questionnaire to identify the level of information literacy competences students possess at the point of entry, and through the self-evaluation of the learning process as a summative task to reflect on the skills developed on completion of the module. It will also raise the students' awareness on the transferability of these competences through future use.

Revised learning outcomes

The learning outcomes reflect an expanded interpretation of information literacy that includes a stronger academic literacy element in addition to the original information literacy competences. In the revised module students are expected to:

1. use essential features of the University's ICT facilities effectively and to develop threshold ICT skills appropriate to HE standards;
2. locate, evaluate, process and present information, using both printed and online formats, that will enable them to interact effectively with their subject disciplines;
3. apply basic research skills to complete a range of academic tasks;
4. evaluate the extent of their learning experience and reflect on this for the purposes of their future study.

Revised assessment

The formative–summative approaches have been retained together with their underpinning rationale:

- The formative diagnostic questionnaire is designed to help students evaluate their own expertise and further development needs and to plan their own progress through the module.
- The summative assessment consists of a portfolio of tasks that encourages the application and transferability of the information literacy skills promoted by this module.

The assessed portfolio consists of four main tasks:

1. Practical ICT tasks demonstrating file management, word-processing skills and effective interaction with online resources; e-mail correspondence with a tutor to illustrate competent use of electronic forms of communication. (Learning Outcome 1.)
2. Plan of study with supported bibliography on a topic taken from another module. Here students will be asked to retrieve information from a variety of sources (e.g. website, book, newspaper article) for the selected topic and to produce an appropriate bibliographic listing. (Learning Outcome 2.)
3. A piece of research on a discipline-specific topic selected by the students in consultation with a tutor. (Learning Outcome 3.)
4. Self-evaluative report reflecting on the student's learning experience, the quality of interaction with the learning resources and the expected

transference of the information literacy skills developed to aid the successful completion of other modules at certificate level. (Learning Outcome 4.)

The single portfolio approach was introduced for two main reasons: primarily to make the assessment strategy as simple as possible, thereby minimising any risk of misunderstanding the requirements to complete this module, and also from a logistical perspective to simplify the level of administration of the work submitted.

Amended syllabus

To accommodate the widened interpretation of information literacy, the syllabus has also been expanded. The main areas of the syllabus are summarised here.

- Definition of information literacy competences and how these help to improve academic performance (including avoidance of plagiarism and of information overload).

In addition to poor information skills, MacDonald (2002) points to factors such as poor time-management and planning skills when exploring the causes of plagiarism. Practice in DASS has shown that plagiarism and information overload feed on each other as students who are unable to filter the information and translate it into knowledge simply quote verbatim from the source. Tutorials on referencing skills will be introduced at certificate level for the first time in 2004 to ensure the development of bibliographic and citation skills and to counteract practices of plagiarism. In addition, a range of online tutorials on academic skills will be available on the ilit.org website to equip students with the necessary critical thinking skills required to interact effectively with the information.[17]

- Independent learning through effective search strategies and evaluation of information. Ability to interact with a variety of information systems, such as OPAC, subject-based electronic resources and search engines. Evaluation of factors such as currency, reliability and relevance of the information gathered for subject-specific topics.

Findings from the content analysis of self-evaluation tasks from previous cohorts have shown that this area of information literacy is crucial to equip students with the investigative skills they need for their academic studies. This is particularly true of mature students.

- Familiarisation with the University's ICT systems – accessing the University network and online facilities to enhance the HE learning experience.

As the University moves towards an e-learning provision, learning resources are increasingly available online, and students need to be introduced to the institution-specific facilities to take full advantage of the services on offer.

- ECDL[18] modules (in intranet and CD-ROM formats) covering four of the seven units. These are:

  - basic concepts of IT,
  - using the computer and managing files,
  - word processing,
  - information and communication.

The University uses the ECDL course-ware[19] as an interactive tutorial to develop basic ICT skills, and practice has confirmed that ECDL is a useful starting point for students with very low competence in ICT. However, the tutorial is far too basic for those with some skills in computer use. In-house material is used to help this group of learners apply their ICT skills beyond the basic interaction with computers and to develop more complex information management skills.

- Introduction to practical skills in the creation and basic design of electronic documents for a range of tasks.

Document design is included to complement the ECDL tutorial as this is only suitable as an introduction to basic manipulation of the Microsoft Office software, while knowing how to apply basic design to documents is an essential attribute of communication and presentation skills.

Bibliography

- Buzan, T. (1995) *Use your Head*. London: BBC Books.
- Dedicated website: *http://www.ilit.org*, information literacy DASS option. This page contains customised learning resources underpinning

the provision of the entire syllabus and providing links to relevant resources, such as the OPAC, the newspaper database and the Athens website, to ensure full immersion in the HE environment.

- Virtual Training Suite: a set of online tutorials designed to help students improve their Internet information skills. Available at: *http://www.vts.rdn.ac.uk/*

- A customised version of the Internet Detective: an interactive tutorial on evaluating the quality of Internet resources.[20]

The book by Buzan is recommended to students as essential reading for the academic literacy element of the module as this was used successfully in the earlier provision of the study-skills programme. Also listed here are essential links with which students will become acquainted during the course of the module. In particular, provision relies on the customised website, ilit.org, which contains a web page dedicated entirely to this module, providing a one-stop-shop approach to access both learning resources and assessment details.

Diagnostic questionnaire – (2004/5)

The changes introduced in the module have resulted in two major alterations of the questionnaire.

- At a structural level two additional sections, referencing and writing skills, have been added to the three original components of ICT, searching and evaluating skills, to address the expanded interpretation of information literacy and to test students' competence in academic literacy.

The questionnaire is shown in full in Appendix F, but note that the example included here is designed in a format that is suitable for the printed medium and therefore lacks the interactive quality of the web-based version. Web access to the questionnaire is available at: *http://www.north.londonmet.ac.uk/mco/surveys/diagnostic.htm*.[21] Students will be able to access this from the ilit.org website as a direct link in order to avoid the problem of having to type long web addresses, which students with poor keyboarding skills find rather cumbersome and unfriendly.[22]

- The method used to assess the students' initial information literacy skills has also altered radically, as questions about the five categories are based on true/false outcomes that measure knowledge of basic information literacy competences and aim to provide a more accurate learning profile. By contrast, the previous version of the questionnaire was based on students' rating of their skills. Practice has shown that this method was open to over-rated skills evaluation by the students, which had a misleading impact on their learning profile.

Examples of questions from the Searching skills section (2004/5):

Using the Internet Explorer's facilities	True	False
By creating a favourite the website's address is saved and can be accessed at a later date	☐	☐
Favourites can be organised into folders	☐	☐
The Refresh button is used to reload a website	☐	☐

Examples of questions from the searching skills section (prior to 2004)

Internet – Please indicate your level of ability in using the following facilities offered by the web browser

Internet Explorer:

	Good	Average	Poor	Don't know
Identifying web addresses	☐	☐	☐	☐
Create favourites	☐	☐	☐	☐

- The content of the questionnaire covers information literacy activities that address the most frequent errors made by previous cohorts in both the information literacy and the study skills modules. Very few students, for example, know how to create a favourite in Internet Explorer and are therefore unfamiliar with the benefit that such a small task generates in facilitating the retrieval of websites. Similarly, the majority of students think that adding a list of references and calling it a bibliography will exonerate them from plagiarism.[23] The assumption made here is that to become information literate students should know how to perform the tasks tested by the questionnaire, and therefore should be able to answer all the questions correctly. Therefore, students will be encouraged to complete the questionnaire at the beginning and at the end of the module to develop a quantifiable profile of their progress.

Summary

Information literacy practice at undergraduate certificate level is one of the hardest to accomplish for a number of reasons. The challenges associated with this type of provision together with strategies adopted to address them are explored in this case study. In the first instance the students do not possess information literacy competences when they begin their degree and such a lack of competences is found in traditional and mature students alike. This picture is supported by the general trend displayed by the diagnostic questionnaires, which shows that most of the students come equipped with some ICT skills, but have little competence in searching and evaluating information for a given task, especially an academic one. The practice presented here shows how poor information literacy was tackled by fostering foundational skills in searching two of the most common academic sources, the online catalogue and the newspaper database. This has produced an unforeseen empowering effect as students' confidence in handling information has increased alongside their familiarity with the sources. The Google search has also introduced searching and evaluative techniques that were not known by the students prior to the module, and the feedback illustrates that these strategies were useful even to those learners with advanced ICT skills.[24] The ultimate aim of this module was to encourage students to transfer their information literacy competences to complete other assignments and comments here show that students took full advantage of being able to access, evaluate and communicate information by applying these competences beyond the confines of the module. There is one final issue raised by some students on the need to embed information literacy beyond the certificate level into advanced subject-specific modules such as the research methodology or the dissertation. The strategy of integrating information literacy at all levels of provision is an issue that needs to be tackled at institutional level and cannot therefore be addressed here. It is encouraging to see, however, that both the frameworks and the learners agree that information literacy should be embedded within the full programme of study and that they consider the research route as the most appropriate way to accomplish this.

Notes

1. The self-evaluation task operates along the lines of the relational model promoted by Bruce (1997), which is explored in Chapter 2, although the research approach adopted here focuses on the students' perspectives, which gives it a closer affinity to the study by Lupton (2004).
2. These include: cultural studies, digital media, health studies, mass communications, media studies, social policy and sociology.
3. In line with the recommendation by Doherty et al. (1999), lectures were selected as the best method of introducing the assessment and access to the web-based learning resources.
4. The web page dedicated to this module is accessed by selecting the information literacy DASS option from the ilit.org website. Further details on this website are found in Appendix K.
5. During the development of this module we experimented with a few other search engines before settling for Google on the basis that this supports the search strategies we intended to cover and has an uncluttered interface. In addition, we have selected the UK version of Google to facilitate the evaluation process by limiting the source of the sites retrieved to the UK.
6. *http://www.sosig.ac.uk/desire/internet-detective.html* (accessed 30 June 2004).
7. Extract from a student self-evaluation. The handbook has now been replaced with web-based handouts to facilitate remote access to the learning resources.
8. The metaphor plug-and-play was taken from the computing term used by Microsoft to describe the process by which the Windows operating system recognises and installs software drivers for hardware devices automatically as soon as these are plugged into a computer.
9. The statistical analysis was produced by the Marketing Department at the University using Snap Survey software, version 7 developed by Mercator, Bristol.
10. This attitude is also reinforced by compulsory attendance employed in other courses.
11. Extract from a student's feedback questionnaire.
12. The student was referring to an access management system academically specific facilities, such as Athens, offering online and remote access to a vast range of subscription databases.
13. This illustrates a clear example of information overload caused by a lack of searching skills required to filter out the irrelevant information.
14. Overall students become particularly confused when faced with the task of finding a chapter authored by X in a book edited by Y. They invariably search for the author of the chapter not the editor when undertaking an author/title search. So the comment from this student illustrates a real sense of achievement.
15. Although curricula of individual subjects include modules covering research methodology skills, these are not shaped by a fully fledged information literacy approach.

16. Prior to 2004 academic literacy came under a separate study-skills programme.
17. These will be available from the information literacy DASS option at the beginning of the academic year 2004/5. Guidelines on how to access the ilit.org website are included as Appendix K.
18. The ECDL (European Computer Driving Licence) is a practical certification designed to equip users with basic computer literacy. It consists of seven modules: basic concepts of information technology; using the computer and managing files; word processing; spread-sheets; databases; presentations; information and communication (this covers e-mail and the Internet).
19. The version of the ECDL tutorial used at London Metropolitan University is provided by Educational Multimedia Corporation, compuTRAINER 2001.
20. The original version of the Internet Detective is available at: *http:// sosig.ac.uk/desire/internet-detective.html* (accessed 10 July 2004).
21. Accessed 11 July 2004.
22. The problem of long and complicated URLs was originally associated with the first Information Literacy website in 2000/1, hosted on one of the University of North London's servers. Its address, *http://learning.unl.ac .uk/uw100/*, was causing problems of access during the induction of the module as students kept either misspelling the address or leaving part of it out. In 2002 a new site was developed and the *http://www.ilit.org* domain was established with funding from LTSN-ICS and SWAPltsn. Students use ilit.org to access the site, and even those who are not confident with computers or have poor keyboarding skills find this address easy to input, primarily because it is short.
23. Extract from the interview with the tutor running the study-skills programme at DASS.
24. Thus confirming the point made by all three frameworks explored in Chapter 3 that ICT skills come under the umbrella term of information literacy because interaction with ICT must be embedded in critical and evaluative skills that only information literacy provides.

Case study 2: Applied Information Research

> [Studies on information literacy are] drawing upon a range of 'user' or 'People-oriented' theoretical frameworks, which are making possible outcomes that are highly relevant to professional practice. Some of these studies are using existing disciplinary basis, such as information seeking and use research, or educational research. [Information literacy research outcomes provide] a source of knowledge relevant to educators, librarians and other information professionals. Work in progress may be loosely categorised as research-in-practice [and] applied research. (Bruce, 1999)

Studies on information literacy offer some insight into its nature and ways of integrating information literacy education within subject-specific curricula. The frameworks explored in Chapter 3 promote the research process as the main route to integration, and the first case study has attempted to illustrate how the fundamental elements of information-seeking competences are used as the basis for information literacy provision at the first-year level of a number of social science courses. In this second case study information literacy is integrated in a much more complex research perspective that suits the needs of postgraduate provision. In addition, the module needs to address the research requirements of information practitioners operating within an information-service environment. In the Applied Information Research (AIR) module, these are contextualised in a user–provider paradigm and evidence-based information practices. The applied nature of information research is therefore investigated through the adoption of an action research perspective in which practice and reflection guide the knowledge construction process. This research route is transferable to other professional subjects, as demonstrated by the integration of information literacy programmes within professionally oriented disciplines at the University, such as law (Andretta, 2001) and social work.[1] The latter development is part of the research-focused and independent learning approach shared by other projects in this discipline. A good example of this is the project entitled: Research Mindedness in Social Work and Social Care, which aims 'to help students and practitioners of social care and social work make greater and more effective use of research in their studies and in practice'.[2]

Information literacy and the information professional

The frameworks promoted by ACRL, ANZIIL and SCONUL describe information literacy from a learner's perspective. AIR also explores the term from an information professional angle, which involves:

> the ability to participate in the development of one's profession and the ability to continuously gather information in one's professional field, ability to develop one's tasks and continually search for data, information and knowledge to fulfil these tasks. (Hepworth, 2000: 24)

The need for librarians, and information professionals in general, to be information literate has been raised by a number of library and information professionals organisations. For example, ALA recommends that: 'Librarian education and performance expectations need to include information literacy' (ALA, 1989). In the ANZIIL framework, Peacock presents the perspective of librarians who operate within the HE environment and argues that: 'the role of librarians is changing as they seek to devise, develop and implement strategies and systems which embed information literacy in the curriculum' (Peacock, 2004: 29). Also commenting from an educational perspective, a report by the Executive Advisory Group to CILIP proposes that information literacy should be integrated as a 'core outcome' (Executive Advisory Group to CILIP, 2002: 28) in all the subjects and at all levels. Taking a wider information professional view this group recommends that:

> CILIP should consider accreditation of courses/modules in advanced information literacy for people going into, or in roles

which require aspects of information specialism – e.g. analysts, market researchers, competitive intelligent officers. (Ibid.)

Initial work on the AIR module was based on the premise that, as the core research methodology unit within the MA of Information Services Management,[3] this was the most suitable module in which to embed information literacy education within lifelong learning and CPD initiatives. These developments were based on a number of considerations. At a generic research level, Bruce claims that postgraduate students need to come to terms with 'the challenges of the information environment' (Bruce, 1997: 10) in order to embrace fully the research culture. Secondly, according to Johnson, programmes such as AIR must be placed within the context of the reflective practitioner, so as to reinforce the connection between 'the skills that learners need to be learners, and those that they need as members of different kinds of communities of practice after graduation' (Johnson, 2003: 48). This is echoed by Schön's more general comment on the need for flexible practice by current professional communities:

> Professionals are called upon to perform tasks for which they have not been educated, and the niche no longer fits the education, or the education no longer fits the niche [...] the situations of practice are inherently unstable [...] professions are confronted with an unprecedented requirement for adaptability. (Schön, 1991: 15)

The MA programme addresses the needs of practitioners who provide information services primarily in the voluntary and public sectors. This is evident from the research focus of the proposals submitted for AIR, where out of a total of 41 scripts, 17 projects came under the category of public library provision, a further 17 covered educational provision ranging from library services operating primarily within HE and FE environments, while the remaining seven proposals focused on topics ranging from the evaluation of the directory enquiry services to the provision of information services in support of carers. As feedback suggests, the development of independent learning skills is particularly relevant to part-time students who are already working as information professionals and who are expected to implement information literacy education in their professional practice. However, in principle the independent learning and evaluative skills fostered by AIR are transferable to the practice of all information communities.

'Librarians are no longer keepers of information, but teachers of information'[4]

In 1991 Rader observed that prior to the introduction of information literacy, librarianship training concentrated on information services 'such as collecting, organising, and accessing information, and offering excellent library services including highly developed user-instruction programs' (Rader, 1991: 28), while information literacy emphasised the facilitation of learning.[5]

> Information-literacy programs will also involve teaching users evaluation of information, problem solving and critical-thinking skills, and librarians have generally not been trained for nor taught these skills. (Ibid.)

Rader concluded that to support information literacy provision:

> Librarians will have to be active learners who use and apply the resources they teach. How and what people are taught regarding the handling of information will become an important part of librarian and teacher training. (Rader, 1991: 27)

Over a decade later Albrecht and Baron's reflections on the impact of information literacy on the profession resonate with the concerns voiced by Rader. In the first instance they are doubtful about the extent and type of approaches adopted by the LIS programmes to help information professionals become facilitators of information literacy training once they qualify. Furthermore, they comment that the type of CPD strategies undertaken by practising librarians should concentrate on instructional skills that conform to the new information literacy and learning-how-to-learn culture. Like Rader, they argue that graduate training in library instruction and information literacy involves much more than simply learning 'how to teach' (Albrecht and Baron, 2002: 73). On the contrary, effective programmes should equip students with competences that ultimately promote lifelong learning where:

> Librarians must be strongly positioned as key educators in the teaching and learning environment, and empowered with an educational competence and professional confidence equal to that of their academic peers. (Ibid.)[6]

AIR in context

The development of AIR was therefore based on two main requirements: the module had to address the needs of practising information communities, and information literacy had to be seen as a fundamental attribute of the profession as a whole. This view is supported by the perspectives put forward by ACRL, ANZIIL and CILIP, and is promoted by Moore as an effective way of ensuring the dissemination of information literacy education.

> Overall, programmes involving teachers and teacher-librarians in authentic learning situations that require intensively doing information literacy, through instructional design and action research, appear to reap the most powerful changes in knowledge and practice. (Moore, 2002: 11)

Integration of information literacy education in AIR was in part motivated by the MA programme's affinity with the library community and the opportunity to influence future practitioners in this field. However, placing information literacy in an applied-research context provides a methodological framework that is appropriate to investigate features from any information sector. A student's feedback on the module confirmed that AIR was seen as:

> Extremely relevant to our future professional practice [as] the need for research and evaluation (evidence based practice) of services and systems will increasingly be a requirement for library and information sciences professionals.[7]

The high degree of relevance can be attributed to the results of widespread consultation with information professionals from a range of information practices who have a long-term working relationship (through the placement system) with the Information Management School. This consultation exercise identified three main competences that employers expect in newly qualified information practitioners: knowledge of information sources, a flexible 'can-do' attitude and good communication skills. This professional profile was complemented by the professional requirements on research competence indicated in the UK-specific literature. The view proposed by Hepworth, for example, was fully endorsed by the AIR module as it confirmed the expectations of the employers consulted.

According to Hepworth, library staff need:

> To broaden their perception of information management to include the management of data. This is becoming increasingly apparent in the digital library environment [and because of this library staff] would benefit from courses in research methodology and experimental practice as well as methods for presenting and visualising information. (Hepworth, 1999)

AIR module outline

The module consisted of two main elements: the applied or action research perspective, and the focus on information research. These elements encouraged the development of practical research skills and the implementation of dissemination strategies that were relevant to and that addressed the needs of information professionals. These aims were achieved in two ways: through the completion of an application for funding a research project and through the dissemination of the project's details using oral and written communication skills. The funded-research environment was chosen because of the combined criteria of quality research and value for money that are applied when allocating funds. This rigorous selection process offered a real world context, as advocated by Breivik (1998) and Bruce (2002), in which to develop effective research skills. In summary, the module aimed to:

- develop information research skills defined as essential competences by information professionals;
- introduce practices and processes of writing a funded research proposal;
- develop competent use of a range of dissemination techniques.

Learning outcomes

By the end of the module students will be able to:

1. design a research project exploring an issue relevant to the information profession in support of an application for funding;
2. identify and evaluate relevant literature in order to contextualise the research proposal;

3. select research strategies appropriate to the nature of the proposed research project;

4. communicate the various aspects of the research project using a range of dissemination strategies.

Assessment details

The assessment consisted of two components: an oral presentation of the proposal and a written application for funding in an area of information management. Students presented the main aspects of the research proposal before the end of the semester and were expected to use appropriate communication technologies to support their presentation (see guidelines, below). To emphasise the reflective approach, this component was assessed in weeks 10 and 11 of the semester. As a result, the students were given formative feedback on their performance, and on the quality of their research project, which they were expected to take into account when writing the final proposal at the end of the module. This component addressed Learning Outcome 4 and was allocated 40 per cent of the total grade.

Guidelines on the presentation of the research proposal

The presentation will last 15 minutes and its structure should cover:

Title of the proposed bid.

Context – here you should set out the scenario for your project based on the review of the literature and your awareness of relevant research that preceded your proposal.

Research design – this should give a clear rationale for the adoption of the design selected, and should cover your aims, outcomes, methodologies and sampling strategies adopted.

Dissemination strategy – this should identify the appropriate strategy for dissemination (i.e. action, awareness) and give details of the intended dissemination outcomes.

Schedule and costing – under schedule and costing you will be expected to provide a rough estimation of time and expenditure required to implement the methodologies, data analysis and dissemination targets.

Your proposal will be assessed according to three criteria: originality, measurability and transparency according to the action research perspective.

The written application for funding outlining a research proposal was a summative assessment that addressed all the learning and was allocated 60 per cent of the total grade. To make this assignment as realistic as possible, a simplified version of the application form from the Arts and Humanities Research Board (AHRB) was used.[8]

Learning and teaching methods

The module was delivered via a series of lectures with additional learning in computer labs and seminars. Also, the online support system was used extensively for formative feedback on the exercises students completed during the course of the module. The online element was used successfully in equivalent information literacy provision. McFarlan and Chandler, for example, state that the online approach contributes to an information literacy spiral that evolves throughout the degree programme, in which 'learning is facilitated through an ongoing series of formal, continuous learning opportunities' (McFarlan and Chandler, 2002: 119).

The knowledge-spiral and action-research approaches

The investigative aspect of information literacy was reflected in AIR through provision that encourages active engagement with a knowledge-spiral process. This, according to Bawden and Robinson, involves the following activities:

> [the] recognition of a need for information; choice of appropriate sources; information retrieval; evaluation of retrieved information; organisation of information; manipulation and processing of information; communication and storage of information; effective use of information. (Bawden and Robinson, 2002: 298)

This model is illustrated as a spiral rather than as a two-dimensional circle because the elevation of the spiral depicts the increase in the learner's knowledge to a higher level of cognition and awareness.

The spiral/cyclical learning process was fully embedded in AIR in two ways:

- Through the syllabus, by combining the knowledge spiral process with an action research perspective, and by contextualising this within the parameters of funded research to emulate a 'real-world situation' and problem-solving based on real conditions (O'Brien, 1998).

- Through the mode of delivery, by following the view of learning promoted by Bruce's (2002) information literacy model, which consists of three main stages: learning, reflection and transfer of learning.[9] Hepworth's key areas of learning covered in the Chapter 2 were also taken into account to ensure an appropriate coverage of information literacy competences suitable to postgraduate research.

Selection of the action research perspective stems from its emphasis on 'learning by doing' (O'Brien, 1998), or experiential learning, which complements the independent learning approach promoted by information literacy. In addition, the investigative practices of the Action Research perspective are based on appropriate theoretical considerations that distinguish it from other types of problem-solving activities. As described by O'Brien (1998):

Action Research aims to contribute both to the practical concerns of people in an immediate problematic situation and to further the goals of social science simultaneously.

A further distinction can be drawn between action research and other types of research as the former promotes an active involvement of those participating in the study and a strong subjective research perspective, although perspectives from other participants in the study are fully acknowledged in the course of the investigation. O'Brien presents the following diagram to illustrate the cyclical nature of action research, in which: 'each cycle has four steps: plan, act, observe, and reflect' (O'Brien, 1998; Figure 6.1).

From a professional point of view the reflective approach promoted by action research is appropriate for practitioners who need to evaluate some kind of service provision, or the implementation of a policy (Robson, 2002). Such a view emphasises the relevance of this approach to information professionals who continually strive to enhance the performance of systems and services. This 'real world' contextualisation of research is complemented by the strategies of experiential learning and

Figure 6.1   The action research cycle (O'Brien, 1998)

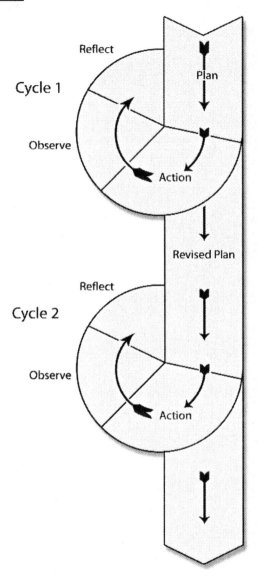

formative feedback as they facilitate reflection on the research activities that students undertake throughout the module. Students' comments confirmed that this reiterative and reflective learning approach led to improved research skills and, most importantly, increased the students' confidence as independent learners. Research strategies that address an action research perspective were therefore fully explored in AIR through the use of formative learning activities. To illustrate how this works in practice general themes from the syllabus are listed here together with the type of tasks that encourage the development of independent learning skills related to the theme explored.

For example, the perception of the relevance of qualitative or quantitative methodological perspectives to information practitioners was encouraged by asking the students to write a short paper assessing either approach. Details of the outcome of this exercise are found in a later section together with an analysis of the students' performance.[10]

Literature review skills were fostered in two ways: at a general level by asking students to apply given evaluation strategies that were suitable to different sources of information, such as books, journal articles and online resources; and at a more specific level by asking students to review a book and a journal paper.[11] The guidelines below outline the review process taking Hart's *Doing a Literature Review* as the focus of the review. This had the dual purpose of encouraging practice in reviewing skills based on a book that is listed as essential reading for AIR.

Book review exercise

Using the structure below write a 1,000-word review of the following book: Hart, C. (2002) *Doing a Literature Review. Releasing the Social Science Research Imagination*. Sage Publications.

Book review structure

Introduction
General description of the book; look at the following information to obtain a general feel of the content

- TOC;
- Summary;
- Introduction/conclusion chapters;
- Index, bibliography;
- Viewpoint taken by the author and resources used.

Purpose of the book

- What are the aims of the book?
- Is the book unique; does it add new information? Is it a useful addition to the literature in this area? (Comparison with similar publications and/or previous editions.)

Evaluation

- Book's strengths and weaknesses;
- Are the themes or arguments well developed?
- Is the audience fully identified?
- Evidence used to support the arguments?
- Has anything been left out?

This type of exercise was an effective way of developing reviewing skills because it further emphasises the real world contextualisation of research activities, as reviewing of books is common in information-based journals from both academic or professional contexts. Secondly, it introduces the concept of writing for a specific audience, which was one of the main aims of AIR. In future this exercise will be complemented by concept mapping[12] and ICT-based archiving activities in response to the problems of knowledge construction and organisation raised by the first cohort of AIR.

The application of sampling and methodology strategies was explored within the funded research context through evaluation of a number of externally funded projects. Below is the example of an evaluation task based on a project funded by the LTSN-ICS.[13]

Assessment of the ilit.org project funded by LTSN-ICS (2002–3)

Read the following documentation for this project: original bid, and both reports submitted in March and August 2003. These documents should provide you with the information required to answer the questions:

1 What research strategies were adopted in this project?
2 What sampling method was used?
3 Were the outcomes of the project fully achieved?
4 What problems did the researcher face?
5 What issues did the students raise?
6 Did the project generate any benefits? If so, what?
7 In your view, was this project successful overall?

The use of strategies for funded research, including the dissemination methods adopted to maximise the impact of the research outcomes, was investigated by asking students to develop a group-based presentation set within the parameters of an application for a mini-project. Details of this task, together with the feedback provided by the tutors, are explored in a later section.

Bibliography

The lists of print and electronic references were kept deliberately short to encourage students' exploration of the online resources available from the AIR web page on the ilit.org website. These were used in conjunction with research-based problem-solving activities set during the course of the module. Feedback from a student showed that the electronic journal *Information Research* was used exactly for these purposes:

> Wilson's website was extremely useful for a 'one-stop shop' approach to articles relating to specific research strategies. Useful at the beginning of the AIR module when asked to research qualitative vs. quantitative strategies, and later during the drafting of my dissertation plan.[14]

Printed resources

- Hart, C. (2003) *Doing a Literature Search. A Comprehensive Guide for the Social Sciences*. London: Sage Publications.
- Hart, C. (2003) *Doing a Literature Review. Releasing the Social Science Research Imagination*. London: Sage Publications.
- Robson, C. (2002) *Real World Research*, 2nd edition. Oxford: Blackwell.
- Schön, D. (2003) *The Reflective Practitioner: How Professionals Think in Action*. London: Ashgate.
- Silverman, D. (2001) *Interpreting Qualitative Data*, 2nd edn. London: Sage Publications.

Online resources

- Andretta, S. ilit.org: information Literacy Gateway, Applied Information Research Option, available at: *http://www.ilit.org*[15]
- Kendall, M. Citing Proficiency Test. Department of Information and Communication, Manchester Metropolitan University. This resource was funded by LTSN-ICS in 2002/3. *http://www.ics.ltsn.ac.uk/*

devfund/Margaret_Kendall.html. Available at: *http://odl.mmu.ac.uk/ public/citing_proficiency_test/index.html*

- Wilson, T.D. *Information Research, an international electronic journal,* available at: *http://InformationR.net/ir/*
- Wilson, T.D. Electronic resources for information research methods, available at: *http://informationr.net/rm/*

Analysis of the results from the diagnostic questionnaire

Previous research (Andretta, 2003) has shown that like their undergraduate counterparts some postgraduate students possessed low independent learning skills. Consequently, the diagnostic questionnaire used at undergraduate certificate level was introduced at the beginning of AIR to ascertain the students' information literacy competences at the point of entry. The most important features of this profile are explored here under the three categories associated with the generic areas of information literacy that structure the questionnaire: ICT, searching and evaluating skills. These are preceded by a general profile of the cohort.

Personal details

The profile generated by this quantitative survey was based on a 100 per cent return rate, consisting of 41 completed questionnaires.[16] Of the 41 students in the cohort, 66 per cent were studying in part-time mode and held a full-time job as professionals in a library or an information-related environment, and 34 students (83 per cent) were female. Eighty per cent of the total had a computer at home but this figure dropped to 63 per cent when asked if they had a connection to the Internet at home, suggesting that one-third of students still relied on the University for online access.

ICT skills

The majority of the students were familiar with the basics of manipulating windows in the Windows environment (100 per cent response), the most common ICT tasks like navigation through a web page or using e-mail (98 per cent said yes to both of these), and 93 per cent could send attachments. However, over 40 per cent could not make a back-up of their work. This is surprising given that to be admitted to the programme, the students must have at least 1 year's work experience in an information-related organisation where activities such as these should be common practice.

When asked about competent use of a browser, the majority of students claimed basic skills such as creating and editing favourites (88 per cent and 75 per cent respectively claimed competence in these activities), but 40 per cent did not know how to organise the favourites into folders, making retrieval of bookmarked sites difficult. Knowing how to organise knowledge and ensure its effective use are fundamental attributes of the information-literate person (ALA, 1989) and it is therefore imperative that students acquire these competences. ICT can help in developing organisational skills through the use of software with archiving facilities, such as Furl,[17] which will be used in future provision to enhance the students' information management skills for web-based sources.

Awareness of the invisible web[18] was low, with 78 per cent unable to access information that is not indexed by search engines or subject directories. This is a worrying trend because students on this programme are training to become information professionals, and lack of familiarity with sources that sit outside the reach of Internet searching tools limits their effectiveness as information providers. Ready-made tutorials, such as Brightplanet.com (ibid.) and the University of California, Berkeley's workshop on the invisible web,[19] offer detailed information regarding this subject. The latter was made available to the AIR students to counteract this problem.

In terms of word-processing skills, use of graphics was less familiar than more common text manipulation tasks, with 39 per cent of students not knowing how to produce a document with graphics, and 44 per cent unable to create charts. Problems with visual and presentation skills were also raised in the formative feedback generated by the presentation rehearsal,[20] which ran early on in the module in preparation for the assessed presentation. A more detailed analysis of the group presentation is included in a later section; however, a comment from a student summarised the impact of this reflective learning process in addressing the need to develop visual and presentation skills:

> The group presentation work helped highlight problems and potential ways of improving visual and oral presentation. Individual presentations benefited from this in terms of [enhanced] delivery.[21]

Searching skills

Given the predominantly library background of the students in this cohort it is not surprising to find that library activities associated with general enquiries scored highly. For example, 95 per cent were able check a borrower's information, make a quick author/title search or a more general keyword search, while 90 per cent could renew library loans and 83 per cent could consult general references. The most striking result here was the lack of familiarity with the Athens facilities by 35 per cent of the students. This is unexpected from a cohort of postgraduate students who have completed an undergraduate degree, or are already working as information professionals. In either case, they should have been competent users of services such as Athens. This figure increased to 38 per cent when the ability to use the newspaper online database was assessed. These data pointed to patterns of information-seeking behaviour that cause concern because they illustrate that the level of interaction with online resources is low, even at postgraduate level. In addition, when combined with the data on the inability to access the invisible web, this created a profile of information-seeking that stands in contrast to the 'knowledge of sources' expected by the employers consulted, and promoted by Hepworth's research. Similarly, Internet searching skills revealed awareness of basic keyword-based searches and phrase searching, but a quarter of the students were unable to use Boolean operators.[22] The lack of familiarity with field searching by 35 per cent of the students is puzzling and suggests that, although the majority were capable of using field searching in an online catalogue (e.g. searching by date scored 80 per cent), they could not transfer this skill to a different searching environment.

Evaluation skills

The majority of the students were able to evaluate information in terms of relevance (80 per cent), and 73 per cent of the students claimed competence in assessing currency and reliability to ascertain the quality of the information, although 40 per cent were unable to use accuracy as an evaluative criterion. Again, this revealed a low level of information literacy among postgraduate students and in particular an inability to evaluate the information critically, as advocated by ACRL and ANZIIL.

Analysis of the students' performance in the short paper exercise

In addition to the diagnostic questionnaire, students were asked to write a short paper on the relevance of a research approach to information practices (see guidelines, below). Although not formally assessed, the purpose of this exercise was two-fold: first, it gave students the opportunity to explore independently the issues related to a specific research approach from an information professional perspective in accordance with the guide-on-the-side approach; and secondly, it complemented the findings of the diagnostic questionnaire by assessing the students' competences in analytical, communication, citation and bibliographic skills in line with the knowledge-spiral approach.

Guidelines on the short paper exercise

Write 1,000 words maximum defining either the qualitative or the quantitative approach to research. You need to assess this approach in terms of its relevance to the information profession and use examples of information research to support your arguments.

The focus of this paper is to define and evaluate one approach (qualitative or quantitative) from the information professional perspective using information research projects (listed on the AIR page of ilit.org) as examples.

This task raised the problem of poor submission rate,[23] which was linked to the reluctance by students to participate in exercises that were not seen as affecting their final grade. This attitude was in direct contrast with the group-based presentation, which was completed by the entire cohort, as this had an explicit bearing on the assessed presentation.[24]

Evaluation of the work assessed a number of competences required to accomplish this task. These came under the information literacy skills that are particularly relevant to information practitioners, and included the ability to:

- work to a given brief;
- cover all the points from the required perspective and use evidence to support these;
- identify the audience and communicate the findings in a style that is appropriate to that audience;
- cite the sources correctly using the Harvard referencing style.

Of the 17 scripts returned only two fully addressed the requirements of the task, analysed one approach from the perspective of information professionals and used appropriate examples. Five students explored both approaches, eight used examples that bore little or no relevance to the profession, and 12 gave examples relevant to information research, but these were not fully analysed. A similar profile emerged regarding communication skills, in which the arguments proposed by 14 students lacked clarity and adopted a colloquial style: the majority used the first person and had a tendency to deviate from the brief. In addition, and perhaps most worryingly given the information background of the students, 16 showed poor referencing skills. These were illustrated by the absence of full reference details for direct quotations and omission of references used from the bibliographic list.[25]

Analysis of the group-based presentation and feedback

The cohort expressed concerns over the assessed oral presentation, as no student could claim competence in this type of dissemination practice. To counteract this, a group-based presentation was introduced mid-way through the module. The group presentation was based on the following sections:[26]

- details of the project team;
- title of the project and brief description of the proposal;
- aims of the research and anticipated outcomes;
- methodology;
- dissemination strategies;
- timetable;
- budget.

Each group was given 10 minutes to present their proposal, including time for questions from the audience at the end.

General problems with students' presentation and design skills

Detailed oral feedback was given to each group at the end of each presentation, based on the input of the tutors as well as that of other students. Included below is a summary of some of the most common mistakes made by students during this exercise.

- Some groups did not introduce the proposal at the beginning of the presentation and some did not provide an appropriate ending, leaving the audience to wonder what would come next.

- As students felt nervous about public speaking they tended to read from their notes. This meant that they could not maintain an active relationship with their audience through eye contact or attentive behaviour.

- Some groups did not use the presentation slides as effective visual props, resulting, for example, in a discrepancy between the content of the slides and what was presented orally.

- Over-use of font style. Some groups over-stressed their points by using multiple forms of emphasis, such as capital letters, large type size, bold and underlining.[27] In particular, students were advised not to use underlining in text because of its association with hypertext links.

- Poor balance between text and white space. Most of the slides displayed too much text, instead of conveying a concise message through the use of keywords or summarised points.

- Lack of consistency in the use of font and colours. Some groups used too wide a range of colours and fonts, which had a distracting effect.

Despite the difficulties raised by this exercise, the groups produced original proposals illustrating a wide range of topics and research interests. These included: 'Careers 4 U' a project promoting the development of online careers resources tailored for the needs of 16–18 year olds; 'Information Orienteering', proposing a series of workshops designed to improve the information orientation skills of deaf and hearing-impaired A-level history students attending a school for deaf children; and 'A comparative analysis of user profiles from three different library environments: academic, legal and public'.[28]

Feedback from the summative questionnaires

A two-stage survey was implemented to capture the students' perspective on their learning experience and their overall impression of the AIR module. The first questionnaire took the form of open-ended questions, and was distributed at the end of the module in December 2003. The second questionnaire was disseminated via e-mail in June 2004 after the students had completed the taught part of the programme. Here the use of e-mail for dissemination purposes, compounded by the timing of the second survey in June,[29] meant that students would not respond if an open-ended structure were used. Therefore, the June questionnaire was primarily based on closed questions, although opportunities to elaborate on these were offered throughout. Analysis of the responses presented here is based on the open-ended comments from both questionnaires to provide an in-depth evaluation of the impact of AIR on the students.

Students' feedback on the AIR module

Feedback from the December questionnaire illustrated that students found the AIR module very challenging for a number of reasons. Lack of familiarity with research practice was often mentioned in the students' comments. This confirms Hepworth's (1999) claim that library staff need to be trained in research and dissemination strategies. Students admitted that they: 'knew nothing at all about [research] at the beginning of [the module]', and felt challenged by 'the [research] terminology [and the selection of] the topic for the bid' as they were concerned about the appropriateness of the focus of the proposal they had selected. Unfamiliarity with the subject, combined with the emphasis on the learning-how-to-learn approach, caused confusion among some students who had not encountered this type of provision before the AIR module. A part-time student, for example, made a comparison between this module and the modules completed in the previous year of study,[30] and found AIR: 'Challenging at the beginning. This was because ilit.org is a different way of learning, that is different from last year'. The direct reference to ilit.org, the website used to support provision, could be construed as confirming the strong association promoted by AIR between research and interaction with the sources of information.[31]

The workload was also problematic for some students: 'To begin with I found the volume of work very hard, as I felt a bit like I had been thrown in at the deep end! [AIR was] difficult although interesting, and once I had found my feet I enjoyed the challenge'. In a cohort where the majority of students were part-time and worked full-time as information practitioners these types of problems might be expected. However, practice has shown that students had a tendency not to engage with the learning activities and resources offered by AIR irrespective of their mode of study. Often the cause for this lack of interaction was a low level of information literacy, and in particular the inability to interact with the information effectively, rather than lack of time. This point was illustrated by the fact that the level of engagement with the learning resources and the reflective activities was highest among part-time students. This group had little spare time but scored highly on motivation, and this appeared to be the key factor underpinning the active engagement with the learning process. The following quote from a part-time student illustrates the importance placed upon access to the resources required to enhance the quality of the research: 'Originality of the research will always be a worry, but the searching of the literature [through ilit.org] has helped identify gaps or current trends'.

The effectiveness of experiential learning was fully acknowledged by the feedback from both questionnaires. When asked to comment on the ability to formulate a research design after completing the module, a student's comment from the December questionnaire illustrated the positive impact of experiential learning in fostering research skills: '[my research design skills have] greatly improved. The practical approach of actually working on a research bid has been helpful'. Similarly, comments from the June questionnaire confirmed the appropriateness of the module's assessment, which resulted in increased confidence in defining the research parameters:

> [The] AIR bid proposal [is] a useful lesson [in] being realistic about the scope/topic [of the research project], so [I] feel more competent than at the start of the semester.

Activities fostering reflective learning skills, generated by formative feedback from tutors, were particularly appreciated by the students:

> The group work and presentation for classroom practice was useful [because it provided] peer reviews and feedback from the tutors, particularly as a trial run prior to the assessment. [I am also] much more confident in structuring a literature review. Having to write a 1,000 word review for the AIR module was a useful precursor to the review of the literature for my dissertation.

Professional relevance of AIR

Feedback from the June questionnaire revealed that contextualising the development of research skills within an application for funding was particularly welcomed by the students as this was seen as relevant to information practitioners compared with a more abstract-based research methodology essay:

> Having to produce a bid proposal with very clear restrictions was a useful exercise, which I can see having a practical use in the workplace, much more so than an essay/unstructured assignment would. I would not have related the two if the assessment had been a more abstract piece of work focusing on the theories and not the practice [of research].

This student, who is from an academic library background, also described the professional impact of developing a research design reflected in the expansion of the level and type of service offered to the users:

> [I am] much more confident having had a practical hands-on attempt at research design, particularly as I have never had any involvement in this type of project due to my current position at work. As a senior library assistant [I] would not necessarily be involved in [supporting] research projects, but having had this experience it is something I could offer to assist with in the future ... the skills acquired (e.g. writing a bid proposal and research design) have been included in my CV.

Since making this statement, the student has taken up a new position as Reader Services Librarian in an academic library where research skills and familiarity with the information literacy perspective will offer 'lots of opportunities for user education'.[32] Other comments reflected the long-term expectations of students who saw AIR as useful for career advancements, and this is illustrated by the comment below from the December questionnaire. In this particular case, however, the short-term application of research skills to complete other modules and to support dissertation work was not acknowledged:

> [In the] short term I don't think I'll use the skills a lot, but [in the] long term when I graduate to a higher level job I think the skills

will be useful; especially the skills of communicating my ideas, which have improved considerably.

Lifelong learning and the transferability of skills

The following comment demonstrated the value of AIR in developing essential lifelong learning skills that underpin the dissertation module:

> I feel that I am still learning in that I am now taking the skills learnt during the AIR module and applying them to a real-life situation, that is my own research for my dissertation. So I think that the two things are linked together and that it was important for me to complete the AIR module first.

Communication, both written and oral, is one area where skills are truly transferable as they reflect the ability to convey ideas within the academic and professional environments. In addition, professionals who operate within a user–provider paradigm need clear communication skills to support their users effectively. When asked to comment on these competences students reported considerable improvement in expressing their views to suit different learning contexts: 'I feel more confident to put my ideas forward [for both] the dissertation and the bid'. Reflective skills are applied when assessing their written communication: 'My writing skills need some work but I think they are competent and have improved with the feedback from tutors'. Self-evaluation was also linked to a better understanding of applying a communication style that was appropriate to specific situations: 'Although I am still working on my "academic" style I do feel that I am more aware of what is expected and appropriate for certain scenarios'.

The balance between providing appropriate levels of feedback to foster reflection and ensuring that students do not become too dependent on the tutor's support is difficult to achieve as this rests to some extent on the tutor facilitating this process, but it also requires the students to take active responsibility for their own learning. The process of self-evaluation was described clearly by the latter part of one student's comment in response to the June questionnaire:

> [The] feedback received from the course tutor was invaluable and perhaps if I am honest there is still a tendency to rely on this feedback more than one's own opinion of work produced, partly

because of the academic status of a 'lecturer' and also because it would be foolish not to take advantage of their experience and knowledge. However, taking on board the feedback received at early stages has enabled me to look out for certain elements in my writing style/quality of work/rigour of research design, etc. that I can identify as requiring revision without having to send it to anyone first. So I would consider this to be a transferable skill.

Effectiveness of the AIR web-based resources

One of the open-ended comments collated from the June questionnaire described the usefulness of ilit.org. The student also pointed out that this site played a complementary role to the teaching, and that, without guidance, an active interaction with the resources would have been difficult. Perhaps this is linked to the initial lack of independent learning skills:

> I've found the ilit.org website to be an invaluable resource. I have used it on countless occasions to check new online journal issues, check for new projects and for advice about implementing a research project. However, I think it is most useful when used to support actual teaching. I'm not sure how useful it would have been without a bit of guidance in its navigation to begin with.

Another comment from the December questionnaire illustrated that the AIR resources supported research-based activities beyond the AIR module, such as: 'Executing the literature search (for the dissertation), engaging with the electronic resources, particularly useful alternative resources on ilit.org [that are] not available on the website [of the University]'.

During provision of the module in 2003/4 the AIR web page consisted of three main areas of resources that supported specific activities in the module, namely information research design and strategies, information research projects, and journals on research.[33] The students were asked to provide comments on these in the June questionnaire, and the main points are explored under each of these headings. One general issue that can be drawn from this feedback is the use of these resources beyond the scope of AIR to gather information for other assignments or the dissertation.

Information research design and strategies section

This section included online resources to help students develop their research project for AIR. Students' feedback illustrated that this part of the site was also used for the dissertation:

> Research Methods Resources was also easy to navigate. I use this section frequently while doing my dissertation as it has wide ranging links to useful sites and has helped me to design my research.

Information research projects section

The second section on ilit.org covered a range of examples of information research projects to give students an indication of the type of research that has been funded in the subjects of LIS and to help them formulate a topic for AIR. When asked to comment on the usefulness of this section, feedback from the June questionnaire confirmed that the original aim was successfully met: 'This is useful to build up a picture of the sort of research that is taking place at the moment, and articles about different projects'. Similarly, another student emphasised the relevance of these project for the AIR assignment. However, the resources were discarded as soon as the module ended, reinforcing the idea that students' interaction with supporting resources is driven by assessment-based needs: 'These were really helpful in preparing the AIR bid and getting ideas. I haven't really used them since'.

Evidence of use of the Information Research projects varied considerably. At one end of the spectrum comments reflected a perspective where these resources were used for the duration of the programme: '[the resources] provided me with a credible selection of projects to inform my own work during the MA'. At the opposite end some students did not take advantage of this section. The following comment showed that the resources for the information literacy projects on ilit.org were consulted instead, as the student's interests came under this general area of research:

> [I] didn't really use these resources as I tended to search the Information Literacy Projects section of the website. Also due to the topic I had selected for the AIR bid proposal assignment, I was more interested in the Information Literacy Projects than general information on research.

Journals in the research section

Not surprisingly, comments about the journals of research available from the AIR web page referred to the usefulness of these resources beyond the AIR module to complete other assignments: 'extremely relevant to the preparation of assessments for the other modules [in the Information Services Management programme]'. The use of these was extended to support activities concerning the dissertation as originally intended: 'I used these in my essays for the course and also for planning the methodology for my dissertation'.

Problems of delivery

The June questionnaire revealed some criticism from part-time students on the timing of the induction to AIR, which occurred at the beginning of the module. According to the feedback, induction should have been timetabled in the academic year preceding the module, as this would have given part-time students sufficient time to become acquainted with the resources in preparation for the assessed research proposal:

> An induction session prior to the start of the module would have been useful. This would certainly have given me the opportunity to explore the various elements of the website and be familiar with its content prior to the start of the term so that I could identify what resources would best serve my particular needs during the module, without having to try and focus on the work required for the module and become familiar with the resources at the same time.

In addition, at the beginning of the semester AIR faced serious logistical and technical problems which had a negative impact on the level of delivery. Not surprisingly, these problems were cited in the December feedback:

> Difficulties with room bookings [caused the] overrun on presentation group work. [This meant that] some sessions were missed although lecture notes were available from the ilit.org website ... again IT problems did frustrate the beginning of the group presentation and [further delayed the start of this exercise].

Prolonged room-booking problems caused the most severe disruption to the module, resulting in the absence of a proper induction to the complex organisation of AIR.[34] This led to a sense of confusion about the ethos of the module: 'Initially there seemed to be some confusion from some students about the nature and aims of the module'. As appropriate lecture facilities were not available from the beginning of the semester students felt that:

> This has resulted in the loss of valuable teaching time, and I do not feel that we have covered the entirety of what the tutor had originally planned in any of our sessions so far. This has meant that we have had to do the exercises which the tutor has set us each week with a minimal amount of guidance. In comparison with other modules, where the tutors have had the time to guide us through the syllabus, the AIR and Dissertation modules have been incredibly daunting due to this.[35]

Feedback from the June questionnaire also illustrated that the sessions missed because of timetabling problems had a long-term effect on the students' ability to apply their research skills:

> A practical session on data analysis would have been helpful. Even though the bid proposal required some outline of analysis in the methodology, I felt this was still a theoretical proposal based on concepts I had read about but wouldn't know how to execute in practice.

The logistical problems outlined here reinforce the importance of using a multiple strategy of delivery where face-to-face is complemented by web-based learning resources and online support. This approach enhances the learning experience as students are exposed to different learning contexts, and, at the same time, it minimises any disruption to the learning continuum, by offering alternative practices of dissemination when more traditional methods fail to deliver.

Summary

Despite the difficulties encountered during the provision of AIR, the recursive approach of information literacy, combined with the reflective model of action research, has enabled postgraduate students to develop transferable research design skills and to target an audience through effective communication, both orally and in writing. These competences were identified as desirable both by the literature and by the information practitioners who were consulted in anticipation of the development of this programme. Students' feedback has confirmed that the assessment strategies reflecting real world conditions were particularly suited to a professionally orientated module such as AIR, where the contextualisation of research skills within the constraints of a 'real' application for funding was perceived as relevant to the students' current and future information practice.

Notes

1. The following project was funded by the Social Policy and Social Work Learning & Teaching Support Network (SWAP-ltsn), 2002–4: Developing information literacy skills for social work students, London Metropolitan University, May 2004, *http://www.swap.ac.uk/about/miniproject6.asp* (accessed 15 July 2004).
2. Research Mindedness is funded by the Social Care Institute for Excellence (SCIE), *http://www.resmind.swap.ac.uk/* (accessed 15 July 2004).
3. The MA is a conversion course accredited by CILIP and delivered by the Information Management School at DASS, London Metropolitan University.
4. Albrecht and Baron (2002: 72).
5. This view is supported by the topics of research selected by the AIR students in 2003. Here the role and impact of the facilitation of learning emerged as a common theme within the context of lifelong learning and social inclusion initiatives (Andretta, 2004).
6. This approach would counteract the problems of collaboration experienced by library staff that are explored in Chapter 2 within the context of the UK-based eLit conferences.
7. Extract from the survey on AIR undertaken at the end of the academic year 2003/4.
8. The guidelines for this assessment component are included as appendices H and I.
9. This model is adopted by ANZIIL (Bundy, 2004) in its embedded information literacy model of integration, explored in Chapter 3.
10. The example of the best paper produced for this exercise has been posted on the ilit.org website and will be used as an example with future cohorts.
11. The guidelines for reviewers used here are a customised version of the guidelines provided by *Program*, a journal published by Aslib (*http://www .aslib.co.uk/program/*).
12. Studies in librarianship training have shown that concept mapping is a useful tool for meaningful learning through the structuring of knowledge, and can be applied to: 'reference situations, instruction and research activities to organise and depict knowledge' (Sherrat and Schlabach, 1990: 60).

13. Andretta, S. ilit.org Information Literacy website designed to develop information handling competences for undergraduate information management students, *http://www.ics.ltsn.ac.uk/devfund/Susie_Andretta .html* (accessed 26 May 2004).
14. Extract from the end of the academic year survey, June 2004. The Wilson website refers to the *Information Research* electronic journal included in the list of online resources for AIR.
15. Further details on the ilit.org website can be found in Appendix K.
16. The questionnaire's results are reproduced in full in Appendix J.
17. Furl stands for File URL and enables users to store, recall, share and discover useful information on the Web. Digital information and documents are archived in a personal directory and information is accessible through a full-text search or by categories, which are created easily. Furl was started in the spring of 2003 by Mike Giles and is self-funded. *http://www.furl .net/index.jsp*
18. Also termed deep-web, this is approximately 500 times bigger than the surface or visible web, *http://www.brightplanet.com/deepcontent/tutorials/ DeepWeb/deepwebwhitepaper.pdf* (accessed 15 July 2004).
19. This is part of a series of Internet workshops developed by UC Berkeley Library, *http://www.lib.berkeley.edu/TeachingLib/Guides/Internet/InvisibleWeb .html* (accessed 15 July 2004).
20. Here students were asked to produce and present a proposal in a team-based scenario.
21. Extract from the end of the module survey, December 2003.
22. With hindsight this question (see question 11 in Appendix J) is not clearly formulated and it is therefore difficult to answer. For example, some search engines, such as Google, default to the Boolean AND; the use of this search engine would therefore automatically include the use of Boolean logic.
23. Seventeen students out of 41 completed this task, a submission rate of 41 per cent.
24. Argyris and Schön (1979) [*The role of failure in double-loop learning*, unpublished memorandum] present an alternative explanation for such a poor response rate. They claim that students' reluctance to engage with the reflective process is associated with the 'fear of failure [and that as a result] researchers must take account of the interweaving of cognitive, affective, and group dynamic effects' (Schön, 1991: 321).
25. A similar study by Kendall and Booth (2003) presents problems of poor citation and bibliographic skills by both undergraduate and postgraduate students at Manchester Metropolitan University.
26. These headings were taken from the application form of the LTSN-ICS Development Fund 2002/3, *http://www.ics.ltsn.ac.uk/devfund/projects0203 .html* (accessed 10 July 2004).
27. For example, one group displayed 'any questions?' on the last slide at the end of the presentation in 72-point type, which had an intimidating effect on the audience.
28. Details of the group-based presentations can be found in the AIR section on the ilit.org website.

29. At postgraduate level this is normally the time of the year when students have completed the taught part of the programme and place all their efforts into the dissertation in time for submission by the end of August.

30. Part-time students complete the MA programme in two years and AIR runs in the second year of the course.

31. In accordance with the general definition by ALA (1989) of information literacy as the ability to locate, manipulate and use information effectively.

32. Student's e-mail correspondence, 9 July 2004.

33. It is anticipated that some restructuring of the web resources will occur in time for the academic year 2004/5.

34. This provides an example of the problems encountered when the administrative apparatus is not fully supportive of information literacy initiatives.

35. Student's e-mail correspondence, 7 October 2003.

7

Conclusion

What seems to transpire from a review of the literature and from practice at London Metropolitan University is that the successful integration of an information literacy policy depends on a number of factors. Top-down initiatives must involve a partnership between HE goals, lifelong learning policies and information literacy strategies. The scenarios of the three countries examined in Chapter 2, for example, present educational policies that aim to address lifelong learning requirements, although the information literacy route, promoted by the USA and Australia, offers the most successful mode of integration in a national learning agenda and in the profile of information professionals. At institutional level success is determined by the extent to which information literacy is perceived as an educational goal, and how far this is complemented by the degree of collaboration between those involved in the provision of information literacy. Both ACRL and ANZIIL argue that this collaboration must include staff with faculty, library and administrative responsibilities. A practical example of such collaboration is demonstrated by the development of the diagnostic questionnaire, described in the first case study, which involved the participation of faculty and library staff, with added input at a later stage from marketing and technical teams to translate the questionnaire into a web-based interactive test. This example, however, is indicative of spontaneous cooperation between staff operating in different departments, rather than being part of a coherent institutional support strategy for information literacy provision.

The two case studies illustrate how information literacy provision at the University was influenced by the three information literacy frameworks. For example, SCONUL's idea of identifying library and IT skills as a foundation of information literacy was used to structure provision at certificate level of the undergraduate scheme.[1] This strategy was applied in recognition of the fact that first-year undergraduate students do not know how to use basic information sources associated with academic work, such as the online library catalogue and the online newspaper database. The impact of this strategy has been positive as the development of these foundational skills has given the students a sense of empowerment and an increased confidence in their abilities to use information effectively. Moreover, feedback from postgraduate students highlights the usefulness of the iterative process advocated by the frameworks in developing competences such as research design and communication skills that were unfamiliar prior to attending the AIR module. Schön also refers to this iterative learning approach when commenting on how students he had observed learned 'to model the unfamiliar on the familiar and to reframe their questions[2] around the changes which resulted unexpectedly from their actions' (Schön, 1991: 201).

This idea of an iterative process is central not only to information literacy as such, but also to the development of information literacy education itself. Indeed, an iterative philosophy of educational development underpins the approach of this book and must do so for any similar project that hopes to provide practical guidance on how information literacy provision may be fostered and encouraged. Although information literacy has a set of relatively consistent pedagogical principles that underlie it, it should be clear both from the general discussion of different national frameworks and from the institutional case studies presented that there is no single right way of developing information literacy provision. Actual practice will vary depending on the national context, the relative engagement of relevant professional bodies, institutional contexts, local conditions, etc. These factors need to be taken into account by any information literacy practitioner when planning new provision or when looking to take existing developments further. Provision of information literacy, which is based on the processes of recursive learning, therefore requires an equivalent process of reflection on practice to be undertaken by the information literacy educator. If information literacy is about learning how to learn, for the reflective information literacy practitioner this necessarily becomes a question of learning how to learn how to learn.

The most basic level of iterative reflection must occur at the level of engagement with the students. This requires that the feedback produced by the students on their information literacy experience is used to review the content of the syllabus, edit the learning resources and amend the assessment strategies as appropriate. The never-ending cycle of practice and reflection is particularly evident from the first case study, in which amendments have been introduced to the assessment strategies, the structure and content of the diagnostic questionnaire, and the learning resources with the aim of facilitating the iterative approach and encouraging students' development of independent learning competences that they could then apply to complete the rest of their degrees. Although the AIR module ran for the first time in the academic year 2003/4, a similar review process has already begun, as the feedback from its first cohort has generated the development of additional activities to address problems raised by the current students. These include the need to improve the visual skills for presentation and knowledge construction purposes, as well as the need for greater emphasis on the information literacy approach as the framework for independent learning, enhancing the role of the reflective information practitioner. That the case studies discussed here are examples of ongoing practice means that they are not given as instances of finished or fixed provision, and although they offer examples of how information literacy may be developed, there is no sense in which they should be seen as prescriptive blueprints.

Although the case studies show both the possibilities and the benefits inherent in a systematic approach to information literacy provision, it is incumbent on the information literacy educator to reflect too on the effects of broader factors which can pose obstacles or difficulties. Although the case studies show what may be achieved there are a number of issues that any guide for practitioners has a duty to highlight and which others will no doubt have to confront in one form or another. Many of these extend outside the scope of this study, but can be touched upon here. They can be grouped roughly under a number of headings.

The first is the general question of student anxiety. There is no doubt that many students are very uncomfortable and even resistant to the pedagogy that underlies information literacy. They can be uncertain how to proceed, slow to start, inhibited in their self-reflection and often resentful at what they can easily perceive as a lack of teacher support. Previous research has shown that this problem, at undergraduate level, can be attributed to the students' expectations of spoon-feeding by the tutor and a consequent inability to interact with the resources independently. Although one might expect these difficulties to arise with undergraduates who have just left school, they are by no means confined to this group. Mature students can just as easily succumb to the temptations of a dependence mode of learning underpinned by preconceptions of what 'doing a degree' should ideally be about, and this can even appear at postgraduate level.

In the second case study, low participation was found in the formative exercises, despite the diagnostic opportunity that these activities offered. Whether this can be attributed to 'fear of failure' (Schön, 1991: 321) needs to be explored further with future cohorts. Despite these difficulties, the information literacy provision examined here has illustrated that this process can be transformative as it increases students' confidence in their independent learning abilities and enhances their competences as these skills are transferred to other learning opportunities, but information literacy tutors certainly need a degree of persistence and the confidence to be able to 'stick with it'.

A direct parallel with student anxiety, and something that very often feeds it, is tutor anxiety. This can have a number of effects and can manifest itself in a variety of ways even with very experienced teachers. There is an understandable tendency for teachers, when asked a question by a student, to give a direct answer. The alternative, inherent in the information literacy approach, of answering the question by supporting students in finding their own answers can be both time-consuming and also feel to teachers as though they are being unhelpful. A high degree of peer support among information literacy educators is useful for sustaining commitment to the underlying philosophy of the programme as well being necessary to avoid the situation in which a student elicits a direct answer from one tutor that another was reluctant to provide.

Teacher anxiety in the face of information literacy extends outside the immediate provision itself. Where the idea of independent learning has not fully permeated the learning culture operating at an institution it can be very difficult to implement an information literacy programme as one part of a course, where all the other elements are delivered in traditional mode. This type of learning environment is perpetuated by the tutors' reluctance to let go of the transmittal mode of delivery and in this respect the concerns raised by some academic librarians, particularly in the UK, over the reluctance by faculty staff to adopt information literacy practices, are justified. The rationale underpinning the transmittal approach is based on the beliefs that learning relies on the dissemination of knowledge from the tutor to the student supported by a lecture–seminar paradigm, that compulsory attendance is essential to help students learn and that highly prescribed assessment strategies assist the students' understanding of the discipline studied. In Richard Paul's view, therefore, students' unwillingness to engage actively with critical thinking practices can be attributed to an academic culture that promotes a complacent and apathetic attitude in the learners: 'It is not primarily students but educators who impede the introduction of critical thinking into college and university classes' (Paul, 1992: 22). The primary reason for this is that critical thinking, and its associated problem solving, is 'effortful' (ibid.: 23) as it offers learning conditions that are uncertain at the outset and that augment the anxiety experienced by the learners. Information literacy can provide the competences needed to deal with the unfamiliar only if the tutor is willing to 'let go' and to step aside into a facilitator role that guides rather than dictates the process of learning. But trying to implement an approach that is based around the basic ideas of information literacy in just one part of the student's educational experience can be akin to introducing a high standard of hygiene in just one ward of a hospital: it is not impossible to do, but its benefits always stand at risk of being subverted once the individual moves elsewhere.

This issue leads directly on to the question of the institutional context. It would no doubt be difficult to introduce information literacy into an institutional environment that was explicitly hostile to its basic precepts. However, institutional hostility can take different forms, many of them covert, unintentional and based on long-standing traditional practices. Although the lifelong learning agenda set by Dearing can feature quite high on institutions' mission statements and other public-face documents, this does not in itself lead to the equivalent institutional knowledge or commitment to see through the changes required to implement it. Where senior educational managers do not have a firm grounding in progressive pedagogy, or the vision or ability to turn their slogans into effective programmes for lifelong learning and the encouragement of independent learners, the development of information literacy itself can be the subject of continual tensions and difficulties at the most basic level. For example, where information literacy encourages students to take responsibility for their own learning and to use teachers as one resource among many others, it is not conducive to this approach to have a generalised compulsory attendance requirement. Compulsory attendance in class no more leads to learning than compulsory attendance in a library necessarily leads to reading. Yet in noting a common association between regular attendance and academic success, and then mistakenly assuming that the first is a cause of the second, many institutions continue to sustain compulsory presence in front of a teacher as a core part of their educational philosophy. No doubt this is in part a traditional residue from the days of direct accountability to the local authorities who provided student grants, but this is a practice that would at least bear reflective re-examination where it is not directly abandoned in the interests of treating students as responsible adults learning how to learn.

Institutional resourcing methodologies often militate against the kind of educational practice that underpins information literacy provision. This is not just a question of recognising that developing resources for students can be very expensive in the short term, but of acknowledging that even in the longer term it will require continuing support. Using the traditional once- or twice-weekly lecture and seminar format as the methodological basis for room allocation and for the calculation of staff workloads is often not suitable where staff engagement in a course does not need to be predominantly in the form of face-to-face contact with students within a fixed timetable slot in a set physical location. Cross-institutional cooperation between teachers, library, computing, administrative and other staff also needs a more adaptive methodological approach to the resourcing of information literacy provision than is sometimes possible under existing arrangements.

The national context in HE also clearly has key effects of what may easily be achieved. The differences between the UK on the one hand and the US and Australian contexts on the other have already been highlighted. However, there is a pervasive conception of what constitutes modern relevance and currency in UK educational practice, which concentrates on 'IT skills' and 'e-learning' as the key innovations, without considering the necessary pedagogical setting for the acquisition of information-handling skills and abilities. In the UK the predominant challenge faced by information literacy provision and the most potentially productive aspect of its intervention is not technical but pedagogical. Set in the context of information literacy, what becomes innovative about e-learning is not the 'e' but the 'learning'.

On the whole, the task of implementing developed information literacy programmes requires in many respects a substantial shift in the learning culture of many HE institutions. This does not mean that individual practitioners and teachers will find it impossible to work within existing constraints, and the two case studies in this book should give a flavour of the kind of enterprise that is possible and the benefits to students that may follow. But those who are committed to information literacy will often need a vision and a considerable degree of fortitude to achieve in practice what it has to offer. It is hoped that this book will make a contribution to that endeavour.

Notes

1. Although in contrast with this model, the competences developed at this basic level of provision include some of the complex information skills that SCONUL associates with more advanced students.
2. This is in line with the 'pedagogy of the question' promoted by Paulo Friere (Bruss and Macedo, 1985: 8) and consisting of a practice that challenges the learners to think critically and to adopt a critical attitude toward the world.

Appendix A

Information Literacy Competency Standards for Higher Education – The Association of College and Research Libraries (ACRL)

ACRL's framework was officially launched in January 2000. The framework consists of five standards, 22 performance indicators as well as a range of learning outcomes linked to these performance indicators to enable the students to become information literate. Full details of this information literacy framework are as follows:

Information Literacy Competency Standards for Higher Education, the Association of College and Research Libraries, A Division of the American Library Association, 2000: *http://www.ala.org/acrl/ilcomstan.html* (accessed 30 July 2004).

A PDF of this document is also available at: *http://www.ala.org/ala/acrl/acrlstandards/informationliteracycompetency.htm* (accessed 30 July 2004).

Standard 1: the information-literate student determines the nature and extent of the information needed

Performance indicators:

1. The information-literate student defines and articulates the need for information.

Outcomes include:

a Confers with instructors and participates in class discussions, peer workgroups and electronic discussions to identify a research topic or other information need.

b Develops a thesis statement and formulates questions based on the information need.

c Explores general information sources to increase familiarity with the topic.

d Defines or modifies the information need to achieve a manageable focus.

e Identifies key concepts and terms that describe the information need.

f Recognises that existing information can be combined with original thought, experimentation and/or analysis to produce new information.

2. The information-literate student identifies a variety of types and formats of potential sources for information.

Outcomes include:

a Knows how information is formally and informally produced, organised and disseminated.

b Recognises that knowledge can be organised into disciplines that influence the way information is accessed.

c Identifies the value and differences of potential resources in a variety of formats (e.g. multimedia, database, website, data set, audio/visual, book).

d Identifies the purpose and audience of potential resources (e.g. popular *vs*. scholarly, current *vs*. historical).

e Differentiates between primary and secondary sources, recognising how their use and importance vary with each discipline.

f Realises that information may need to be constructed with raw data from primary sources.

3. The information-literate student considers the costs and benefits of acquiring the needed information.

Outcomes include:

a Determines the availability of needed information and makes decisions on broadening the information seeking process beyond local resources (e.g. interlibrary loan; using resources at their locations; obtaining images, videos, text or sound).

b Considers the feasibility of acquiring a new language or skill (e.g. foreign or discipline-based) in order to gather needed information and to understand its context.

c Defines a realistic overall plan and timeline to acquire the needed information.

4. The information-literate student re-evaluates the nature and extent of the information need.

Outcomes include:

a Reviews the initial information need to clarify, revise or refine the question.

b Describes criteria used to make information decisions and choices.

Standard 2: the information-literate student accesses needed information effectively and efficiently

Performance indicators:

1. The information-literate student selects the most appropriate investigative methods or information retrieval systems for accessing the needed information.

Outcomes include:

a Identifies appropriate investigative methods (e.g. laboratory experiment, simulation, fieldwork).

b Investigates benefits and applicability of various investigative methods.

c Investigates the scope, content and organisation of information retrieval systems.

d Selects efficient and effective approaches for accessing the information needed from the investigative method or information retrieval system.

2. The information-literate student constructs and implements effectively designed search strategies.

Outcomes include:

a Develops a research plan appropriate to the investigative method.

b Identifies keywords, synonyms and related terms for the information needed.

c Selects controlled vocabulary specific to the discipline or information retrieval source.

d Constructs a search strategy using appropriate commands for the information retrieval system selected (e.g. Boolean operators, truncation and proximity for search engines; internal organisers such as indexes for books).

e Implements the search strategy in various information retrieval systems using different user interfaces and search engines, with different command languages, protocols and search parameters.

f Implements the search using investigative protocols appropriate to the discipline.

3. The information-literate student retrieves information online or in person using a variety of methods.

Outcomes include:

a Uses various search systems to retrieve information in a variety of formats.

b Uses various classification schemes and other systems (e.g. call number systems or indexes) to locate information resources within the library or to identify specific sites for physical exploration.

c Uses specialised online or in-person services available at the institution to retrieve information needed (e.g. interlibrary loan/document delivery, professional associations, institutional research offices, community resources, experts and practitioners).

d Uses surveys, letters, interviews and other forms of inquiry to retrieve primary information.

4. The information-literate student refines the search strategy if necessary.

Outcomes include:

a   Assesses the quantity, quality and relevance of the search results to determine whether other information retrieval systems or investigative methods should be used.

b   Identifies gaps in the information retrieved and determines if the search strategy should be revised.

c   Repeats the search using the revised strategy as necessary.

5. The information-literate student extracts, records and manages the information and its sources.

Outcomes include:

a   Selects among various technologies the most appropriate one for the task of extracting the needed information (e.g. copy/paste software functions, photocopier, scanner, audio/visual equipment or exploratory instruments).

b   Creates a system for organising the information.

c   Differentiates between the types of sources cited and understands the elements and correct syntax of a citation for a wide range of resources.

d   Records all pertinent citation information for future reference.

e   Uses various technologies to manage the information selected and organised.

Standard 3: the information-literate student evaluates information and its sources critically and incorporates selected information into his or her knowledge base and value system

Performance indicators:

1. The information-literate student summarises the main ideas to be extracted from the information gathered.

Outcomes include:

a   Reads the text and selects main ideas.

b   Restates textual concepts in his/her own words and selects data accurately.

c   Identifies verbatim material that can be then appropriately quoted.

2. The information-literate student articulates and applies initial criteria for evaluating both the information and its sources.

Outcomes include:

a Examines and compares information from various sources to evaluate reliability, validity, accuracy, authority, timeliness and point of view or bias.

b Analyses the structure and logic of supporting arguments or methods.

c Recognises prejudice, deception or manipulation.

d Recognises the cultural, physical or other context within which the information was created and understands the impact of context on interpreting the information.

3. The information-literate student synthesises main ideas to construct new concepts.

Outcomes include:

a Recognises interrelationships among concepts and combines them into potentially useful primary statements with supporting evidence.

b Extends initial synthesis, when possible, at a higher level of abstraction to construct new hypotheses that may require additional information.

c Uses computer and other technologies (e.g. spreadsheets, databases, multimedia and audio or visual equipment) for studying the interaction of ideas and other phenomena.

4. The information-literate student compares new knowledge with prior knowledge to determine the value added, contradictions or other unique characteristics of the information.

Outcomes include:

a Determines whether information satisfies the research or other information need.

b Uses consciously selected criteria to determine whether the information contradicts or verifies that used from other sources.

c Draws conclusions based upon information gathered.

d Tests theories with discipline-appropriate techniques (e.g. simulators, experiments).

e Determines probable accuracy by questioning the source of the data, the limitations of the information gathering tools or strategies, and the reasonableness of the conclusions.

f Integrates new information with previous information or knowledge.

g Selects information that provides evidence for the topic.

5. The information-literate student determines whether the new knowledge has an impact on the individual's value system and takes steps to reconcile differences.

Outcomes include:

a Investigates differing viewpoints encountered in the literature.

b Determines whether to incorporate or reject viewpoints encountered.

6. The information-literate student validates understanding and interpretation of the information through discourse with other individuals, subject-area experts and/or practitioners.

Outcomes include:

a Participates in classroom and other discussions.

b Participates in class-sponsored electronic communication forums designed to encourage discourse on the topic (e.g. e-mail, bulletin boards, chat rooms).

c Seeks expert opinion through a variety of mechanisms (e.g. interviews, e-mail, listservs).

7. The information-literate student determines whether the initial query should be revised.

Outcomes include:

a Determines if original information need has been satisfied or if additional information is needed.

b Reviews search strategy and incorporates additional concepts as necessary.

c Reviews information retrieval sources used and expands to include others as needed.

Standard 4: the information-literate student, individually or as a member of a group, uses information effectively to accomplish a specific purpose.

Performance indicators:

1. The information-literate student applies new and prior information to the planning and creation of a particular product or performance.

   Outcomes include:

   a Organises the content in a manner that supports the purposes and format of the product or performance (e.g. outlines, drafts, storyboards).

   b Articulates knowledge and skills transferred from prior experiences to planning and creating the product or performance.

   c Integrates the new and prior information, including quotations and paraphrasing, in a manner that supports the purposes of the product or performance.

   d Manipulates digital text, images and data, as required, transferring them from their original locations and formats to a new context.

2. The information-literate student revises the development process for the product or performance.

   Outcomes include:

   a Maintains a journal or log of activities related to the information seeking, evaluating and communicating process.

   b Reflects on past successes, failures and alternative strategies.

3. The information-literate student communicates the product or performance effectively to others.

   Outcomes include:

   a Chooses a communication medium and format that best supports the purposes of the product or performance and the intended audience.

   b Uses a range of information technology applications in creating the product or performance.

c Incorporates principles of design and communication.

d Communicates clearly and with a style that supports the purposes of the intended audience.

Standard 5: the information-literate student understands many of the economic, legal and social issues surrounding the use of information and accesses and uses information ethically and legally

Performance indicators:

1. The information-literate student understands many of the ethical, legal and socio-economic issues surrounding information and information technology.

   Outcomes include:

   a Identifies and discusses issues related to privacy and security in both print and electronic environments.

   b Identifies and discusses issues related to free *vs.* fee-based access to information.

   c Identifies and discusses issues related to censorship and freedom of speech.

   d Demonstrates an understanding of intellectual property, copyright and fair use of copyrighted material.

2. The information-literate student follows laws, regulations, institutional policies and etiquette related to the access and use of information resources.

   Outcomes include:

   a Participates in electronic discussions following accepted practices (e.g. 'Netiquette').

   b Uses approved passwords and other forms of identification for access to information resources.

   c Complies with institutional policies on access to information resources.

    d Preserves the integrity of information resources, equipment, systems and facilities.

    e Legally obtains, stores, and disseminates text, data, images or sounds.

    f Demonstrates an understanding of what constitutes plagiarism and does not represent work attributable to others as his/her own.

    g Demonstrates an understanding of institutional policies related to research on human subjects.

3. The information-literate student acknowledges the use of information sources in communicating the product or performance.

Outcomes include:

    a Selects an appropriate documentation style and uses it consistently to cite sources.

    b Posts permission-granted notices, as required, for copyrighted material.

Appendix B

The Australian and New Zealand Information Literacy Framework: principles, standards and practice (ANZIIL)

The original Information Literacy Standards devised by the Council of Australian University Librarians were developed in 2001 from the American Information Literacy Standards with ALA's full consent. The first edition of the framework was disseminated nationally among faculty and information practitioners with the aim of collating widespread feedback that would inform on the effectiveness of this framework. Following on from this, amendments were incorporated in the current second edition – the Australian and New Zealand Information Literacy Framework: principles, standards and practice – published in 2004. The main difference between the ACRL and the ANZIIL models is the addition of one extra standard in the Australian version. Full details of this information literacy framework are as follows:

Australian and New Zealand Information Literacy Framework: principles, standards and practice, second edition, Bundy, A. (ed.), Adelaide, 2004.

A PDF version can be found at: *http://www.caul.edu.au/info-literacy/ infoliteracyframework.pdf* (accessed 20 July 2004).

Standard 1: the information-literate person recognises the need for information and determines the nature and extent of the information needed

Learning outcomes – the information-literate person:

1. Defines and articulates the information need.

   i. Explores general information sources to increase familiarity with the topic.

   ii. Identifies key concepts and terms in order to formulate and focus the questions.

   iii. Defines or modifies the information need to achieve a manageable focus.

   iv. May confer with others to identify a research topic or other information need.

2. Understands the purpose, scope and appropriateness of a variety of information sources.

   i. Understands how information is organised and disseminated, recognising the context of the topic in the discipline.

   ii. Differentiates between, and values, the variety of potential sources of information.

   iii. Differentiates between the intended purpose and audience of potential resources, e.g. popular *vs.* scholarly, current *vs.* historical.

   iv. Differentiates between primary and secondary sources, recognising how their use and importance vary with each discipline.

3. Re-evaluates the nature and extent of the information need.

   i. Reviews the initial information need to clarify, revise or refine the question.

   ii. Articulates and uses criteria to make information decisions and choices.

4. Uses diverse sources of information to inform decisions.

   i. Understands that different sources will present different perspectives.

ii. Uses a range of sources to understand the issues.

iii. Uses information for decision making and problem solving.

Standard 2: the information-literate person finds needed information effectively and efficiently

Learning outcomes – the information-literate person:

1. Selects the most appropriate methods or tools for finding information.

    i. Identifies appropriate investigative methods, e.g. laboratory experiment, simulation, fieldwork.

    ii. Investigates benefits and applicability of various investigative methods.

    iii. Investigates the scope, content and organisation of information access tools.

    iv. Consults with librarians and other information professionals to help identify information access tools.

2. Constructs and implements effective search strategies.

    i. Develops a search plan appropriate to the investigative method.

    ii. Identifies keywords, synonyms and related terms for the information needed.

    iii. Selects appropriate controlled vocabulary or a classification specific to the discipline or information access tools.

    iv. Constructs and implements a search strategy using appropriate commands.

    v. Implements the search using investigative methodology appropriate to the discipline.

3. Obtains information using appropriate methods.

    i. Uses various information access tools to retrieve information in a variety of formats.

    ii. Uses appropriate services to retrieve information needed, e.g. document delivery, professional associations, institutional research offices, community resources, experts and practitioners.

    iii. Uses surveys, letters, interviews and other forms of inquiry to retrieve primary information.

4. Keeps up-to-date with information sources, information technologies, information access tools and investigative methods.

    i. Maintains awareness of changes in information and communications technology.

    ii. Uses alert/current awareness services.

    iii. Subscribes to listservs and discussion groups.

    iv. Habitually browses print and electronic sources.

Standard 3: the information-literate person critically evaluates information and the information seeking process

Learning outcomes – the information-literate person:

1. Assesses the usefulness and relevance of the information obtained.

    i. Assesses the quantity, quality and relevance of the search results to determine whether other information access tools or investigative methods should be used.

    ii. Identifies gaps in the information retrieved and determines if the search strategy should be revised.

    iii. Repeats the search using the revised strategy as necessary.

2. Defines and applies criteria for evaluating information.

    i. Examines and compares information from various sources to evaluate reliability, accuracy, authority, timeliness and point of view or bias.

    ii. Analyses the structure and logic of supporting arguments or methods.

    iii. Recognises the cultural, physical or other context within which the information was created and understands the impact of context on interpreting the information.

    iv. Recognises and understands own biases and cultural context.

3. Reflects on the information seeking process and revises search strategies as necessary.

    i. Determines if the original information need has been satisfied or if additional information is needed.

    ii. Reviews the search strategy.

    iii. Reviews information access tools used and expands to include others as required.

    iv. Recognises that the information search process is evolutionary and non-linear.

Standard 4: the information-literate person manages information collected or generated

Learning outcomes – the information-literate person:

1. Records information and its sources.

    i. Organises the content in a manner that supports the purposes and format of the product, e.g. outlines, drafts, storyboard.

    ii. Differentiates between the types of sources cited and understands the elements and correct citation style for a wide range of resources.

    iii. Records all pertinent citation information for future reference and retrieval.

2. Organises (orders/classifies/stores) information.

    i. Compiles references in the required bibliographic format.

    ii. Creates a system for organising and managing the information obtained, e.g. EndNote, card files.

Standard 5: the information-literate person applies prior and new information to construct new concepts or create new understandings

Learning outcomes – the information literate person:

1. Compares and integrates new understanding with prior knowledge to determine the value added, contradictions or other unique characteristics of the information.

    i. Determines whether information satisfies the research or other information need and whether the information contradicts or verifies information used from other sources.

    ii. Recognises interrelationships between concepts and draws conclusions based upon information gathered.

    iii. Selects information that provides evidence for the topic and summarises the main ideas extracted from the information gathered.

    iv. Understands that information and knowledge in any discipline is in part a social construction and is subject to change as a result of ongoing dialogue and research.

    v. Extends initial synthesis at a higher level of abstraction to construct new hypotheses.

2. Communicates knowledge and new understandings effectively.

    i. Chooses a communication medium and format that best supports the purposes of the product and the intended audience.

    ii. Uses a range of appropriate IT applications in creating the product.

    iii. Incorporates principles of design and communication appropriate to the environment.

    iv. Communicates clearly and in a style to support the purposes of the intended audience.

Standard 6: the information-literate person uses information with understanding and acknowledges cultural, ethical, economic, legal, and social issues surrounding the use of information

Learning outcomes – the information literate person:

1. Acknowledges cultural, ethical and socio-economic issues related to access to, and use of, information.

    i. Identifies and can articulate issues related to privacy and security in the print and electronic environments.

    ii. Identifies and understands issues related to censorship and freedom of speech.

    iii. Understands and respects indigenous and multicultural perspectives of using information.

2. Recognises that information is underpinned by values and beliefs.

    i. Identifies whether there are differing values that underpin new information or whether information has implications for personal values and beliefs.

    ii. Applies reasoning to determine whether to incorporate or reject viewpoints encountered.

    iii. Maintains an internally coherent set of values informed by knowledge and experience.

3. Conforms with conventions and etiquette related to access to, and use of, information.

    i. Demonstrates an understanding of what constitutes plagiarism and correctly acknowledges the work and ideas of others.

    ii. Participates in electronic discussions following accepted practices, e.g. Netiquette.

4. Legally obtains, stores and disseminates text, data, images or sounds.

    i. Understands fair dealing in respect of the acquisition and dissemination of educational and research materials.

    ii. Respects the access rights of all users and does not damage information resources.

    iii. Obtains, stores and disseminates text, data, images or sounds in a legal manner.

    iv. Demonstrates an understanding of intellectual property, copyright and fair use of copyrighted material.

Appendix C

The Society of College, National and University Libraries (SCONUL) Information Skills model

SCONUL's position paper on Information Skills in Higher Education was produced in December 1998 to initiate a debate on the role of information skills within the HE environment. The resulting Information Skills model is composed of seven information literacy competences supported by basic library and IT skills.

Full details of this information skills model can be found at: *http://www.sconul.ac.uk/activities/inf_lit/papers/seven_pillars.html* (accessed 20 July 2004).

SCONUL seven pillars of information skills

The seven headline skills:

1. The ability to recognise a need for information.
2. The ability to distinguish ways in which the information 'gap' may be addressed:

    i. knowledge of appropriate kinds of resources, both print and non-print;
    ii. selection of resources with 'best fit' for the task at hand;
    iii. the ability to understand the issues affecting accessibility of sources.

3. The ability to construct strategies for locating information:

    i. to articulate information need to match against resources;

    ii. to develop a systematic method appropriate for the need;

    iii. to understand the principles of construction and generation of databases.

4. The ability to locate and access information:

    i. to develop appropriate searching techniques (e.g. use of Boolean);

    ii. to use communication and information technologies, including those of international academic networks;

    iii. to use appropriate indexing and abstracting services, citation indexes and databases;

    iv. to use current awareness methods to keep up-to-date.

5. The ability to compare and evaluate information obtained from different sources:

    i. awareness of bias and authority issues;

    ii. awareness of the peer-review process of scholarly publishing;

    iii. appropriate extraction of information matching the information need.

6. The ability to organise, apply and communicate information to others in ways appropriate to the situation:

    i. to cite bibliographic references in project reports and theses;

    ii. to construct a personal bibliographic system;

    iii. to apply information to the problem at hand;

    iv. to communicate effectively using the appropriate medium;

    v. to understand issues of copyright and plagiarism.

7. The ability to synthesise and build upon existing information, contributing to the creation of new knowledge.

Appendix D

Examples of the application of ACRL standards in different disiplines[1]

Sample outcome by discipline	Correlated ACRL information literacy standard[2]
English Students should be familiar with a variety of linguistic, stylistic and generic conventions	ACRL: 3, 2, 4 4 Recognises the cultural, physical or other contexts within which the information was created and understands the impact of context on interpreting information This standard helps to address evaluative and analytical goals by specifying the differentiation of information resources within the context of various intellectual schema, e.g. culture, time and knowledge arena
History Students should be able to analyse primary-source data including photographs and maps	ACRL: 1, 2, 5–6 5 Differentiates between primary and secondary sources, recognising how their use and importance vary with each discipline 6 Realises that information may need to be constructed with raw data from primary sources Document-based inquiry is accommodated in the standards by recognition of value in research materials derived from a variety of primary and secondary resources

Sample outcome by discipline	Correlated ACRL information literacy standard[2]
Maths Students should be able to represent mathematical ideas via, as well as understand ideas expressed as, pictures, models and diagrams	ACRL: 4, 1, 4 4 Manipulates digital text, images and data, as required, transferring them from their original locations and formats to a new context The standards provide for the synthesis and re-interpretation of new and prior knowledge in non-textual formats appropriate to the content
Science Students should be able to describe and conduct scientific inquiry, defined as the ability to ask a question, and compare their own answers to given answers/knowledge	ACRL: 3, 4, 1–7 1 Determines whether information satisfies the research or other information need 2 Uses consciously selected criteria to determine whether the information contradicts or verifies information used from other sources 3 Draws conclusions based upon information gathered 4 Tests theories with discipline-appropriate techniques (e.g. simulators, experiments) 5 Determines probable accuracy by questioning the source of the data, the limitations of the information gathering tools or strategies and the reasonableness of the conclusions 6 Integrates new information with previous information or knowledge 7 Selects information that provides evidence for the topic using the research process to probe the validity of hypothesis and conclusions addressed by the repetitive, multi-step process described in the standards

Sample outcome by discipline	Correlated ACRL information literacy standard[2]
Visual arts Students should be able to describe and use a range of techniques for producing visual materials	ACRL: 4, 3, 1–4 1 Chooses a communication medium and format that best supports the purposes of the product or performance and the intended audience 2 Uses a range of IT applications in creating the product or performance 3 Incorporates principles of design and communication 4 Communicates clearly and with a style that supports the purposes of the intended audience Consideration of design elements and format of communication mode is prescribed in the standards for effective information transfer to a desired audience

Notes

1. Extract from Booth and Fabian (2002: 138).
2. The notation system is as follows: Standard number followed by Performance indicator number and outcome number. The learning outcome or outcomes have been displayed in full to illustrate how discipline-specific requirements are translated into practical learning outcomes.

Appendix E

The Information Literacy IQ (Institutional Quotient) Test

This IQ test is designed to help you determine the readiness of your institution in integrating information literacy into your curriculum. Respond to each statement by marking it true or false. Total all the number of true statements your have marked and compare your rating with the chart (shown below).

	True	False
Librarians at your institution		
Librarians are teachers at my institution.	☐	☐
Librarians are engaged in curriculum planning (i.e. serve on institutional curriculum committees)	☐	☐
Recognition of the importance of information literacy		
My campus has developed a definition of information literacy	☐	☐
Information literacy is evident in our campus planning documents, such as strategic plans	☐	☐
University administrators are committed to the importance of information literacy	☐	☐
Faculty accept/partake in responsibility for information literacy education	☐	☐
There are support and rewards for faculty who develop and redesign curricula to include concepts of information literacy	☐	☐
Learning/teaching environment		
My campus has developed a definition of information literacy	☐	☐

	True	False
Information literacy is evident in our campus planning documents, such as strategic plans	☐	☐
University administrators are committed to the importance of information literacy	☐	☐
Faculty accept/partake in responsibility for information literacy education	☐	☐
There are support and rewards for faculty who develop and redesign curricula to include concepts of information literacy	☐	☐
Learning/teaching environment		
My institution engages in resource-based, problem-solving learning	☐	☐
My campus encourages a climate of collaboration	☐	☐
Teaching modalities are student-centred (with an emphasis on active learning)	☐	☐
Collaboration exists among curricula designers, faculty, librarians, academic advisors and computing staff	☐	☐
Information infrastructure		
Campus is fully networked	☐	☐
Library offers a variety of digital and print information resources in quantity and scope	☐	☐

Scoring guidelines for the IQ test

Your IQ score (sum of all the statements you marked true) provides you with a relative ranking of where your institution may be in terms of developing an information literacy programme. The following chart is prepared to assist you in moving your institution forward with an information literacy programme, based on your IQ score.

If your total score is:

0–3 You are taking 'first steps'

■ Why not initiate a local discussion with librarians and faculty about the role of information literacy on your campus?

- Invite a librarian/faculty member from a model programme to assist you in beginning a discussion.
- Identify and share some articles on information literacy.
- Look at selected websites on information literacy.
- Identify your regional accreditation requirements for information literacy.

4–6 You are 'on your way'

- Why not form a campus committee or utilize an existing committee, such as a teaching, learning and technology roundtable, to address information literacy?
- Define information literacy.
- Develop a programme proposal for information literacy.
- Identify faculty–librarian development opportunities or propose them.

7–9 You are 'experimenting'

- Why not implement a pilot information literacy programme?
- Examine 'best practices' at institutions similar to your own.
- Construct an assessment tool.
- Consider scalability.

10–11 You are 'full speed ahead'

- Why not consider establishing a fully developed information literacy programme?
- Provide an evaluation of the pilot programme.
- Clearly articulate the goals of a fully developed information literacy programme to faculty and students alike.
- Construct a mechanism for continual evaluation and renewal.

12+ You have a 'model programme'

- Why not consider sharing your information literacy programme as a model?

- Give a paper at a professional meeting (e.g. AAHE, EDUCOM, CAUSE, a conference in a discipline).
- Maintain a website that is linked to that of the Institute for Information Literacy.
- Publicise your success and share your experiences.

Appendix F

Diagnostic Questionnaire 2004/5

Name: ID Number:

Module: Degree:

Mode of Study:	PT	☐	FT	☐	(Please tick as appropriate)

Please tick as appropriate	Male:	☐	Female:	☐

Which age group do you belong to? (Please tick as appropriate)

18–19	20–29	30–39	40–49	50–59	60+

Have you ever used a computer? (If you have answered *no* you will need to complete only the writing skills section of this questionnaire.)

Yes	☐	No	☐

Do you have access to the following? Please tick as appropriate.

	Yes	No		Yes	No
Computer at home	☐	☐	Computer at work	☐	☐
Internet at home	☐	☐	Internet at work	☐	☐

ICT skills

Can you use the following facilities in the Windows environment? (NB If you don't know the meaning of the terms used in this section then select the no option.)

	Yes	No		Yes	No
Open a window	☐	☐	Copy files to folders	☐	☐
Resize a window	☐	☐	Copy files to a floppy disk	☐	☐
Minimise a window	☐	☐	Navigate in Windows NT Explorer	☐	☐
Maximise a window	☐	☐	Copy from one floppy disk to another	☐	☐
Manage folders	☐	☐	Print a word-processed document	☐	☐
Use e-mail	☐	☐	Attach a file to an e-mail message	☐	☐
Format a floppy disk	☐	☐			

Using Internet Explorer's facilities	True	False
By creating a favourite the website's address is saved and can be accessed at a later date	☐	☐
Favourites can be renamed for easy retrieval	☐	☐
Favourites can be organised into folders	☐	☐
The Back button is the same as the Home button	☐	☐
The Refresh button is used to reload a website	☐	☐
Bulletin boards are the same as mailing lists	☐	☐
A mailing list allows you to send the same message to a number of people simultaneously	☐	☐

Using Internet Explorer's facilities	True	False
Sending an e-mail composed of text all in capital letters is regarded as 'shouting' and should be avoided	☐	☐
Rules of grammar, punctuation and style do not apply to e-mails	☐	☐

Searching skills

Internet searching	True	False
Stop words are short and frequently occurring words such as 'the', 'on', 'in', 'of' that are often ignored by the search engine when used in a search	☐	☐
Search engines find websites by trying to match the words contained in the search box	☐	☐
Search engines list sites found by ranking their relevance to the search	☐	☐
To complete a phrase search you need to enclose the keywords in quotation marks	☐	☐
Phrase searching means that all the keywords are searched as a single entity	☐	☐
The term OR is used to retrieve sites that feature any of the terms in the search box	☐	☐
The term AND is used to combine two terms together so that the search engine retrieves sites containing both terms (although these are not necessarily placed sequentially)	☐	☐
Incorrect spelling in a search will limit your searching and may even produce a zero search result	☐	☐
The search engine will automatically correct your spelling when you make a mistake	☐	☐
Some of the search engines allow you to limit the search by date	☐	☐
You can search for images on the Internet	☐	☐

Library and database searching	True	False
You can find journals using the online library catalogue	☐	☐
You can order items from other libraries using the University's catalogue	☐	☐
The library has CD-ROM versions of all newspaper editions from the last 50 years	☐	☐
You need to know the exact title of a book in order to find it by using the online catalogue	☐	☐
Corporate authorship means that an item is written by an organisation	☐	☐

Evaluating skills

Evaluating	True	False
All the information published on the Internet is sound	☐	☐
You can always tell who published a site by looking at the domain name	☐	☐
The URL is the address of the site	☐	☐
To see if a book is relevant you need to read it from cover to cover	☐	☐
Skim reading is when you read the whole text very quickly	☐	☐
Scan reading involves only reading key sections, such as first and last paragraphs	☐	☐
All information found on a university website is academically sound	☐	☐
Websites are always more up to date than periodicals	☐	☐
Articles published in academic journals are not as reliable as books	☐	☐
To evaluate a website you just need to check the date it was produced	☐	☐

Referencing skills

Referencing	True	False
A bibliography is required for every academic essay	☐	☐
A bibliography is the same as a list of references	☐	☐
A bibliography should include references to lecture notes	☐	☐
The Harvard and Vancouver referencing systems are accepted at London Metropolitan University	☐	☐
If you have a bibliography you cannot be accused of plagiarism	☐	☐
If you don't quote directly from a text you don't require a reference	☐	☐
Copyright is the right to copy from books, articles and you can do whatever you want with this information	☐	☐
Direct quotations must be enclosed in 'inverted commas'	☐	☐
You can copy and paste information found on the Internet without having to reference it because the Internet is not protected by copyright	☐	☐
Authors must be listed alphabetically in a bibliography	☐	☐
A site address alone is acceptable as a reference in a bibliography	☐	☐
To find the following item: Scott, J. The old boy network in Giddens, A. (ed.) 2001 *Sociology Introductory Readings*, you need to search for Scott in the Author field	☐	☐
The following is a reference for a book: Carlson, R., Repman, J. Building blocks of Information Literacy, *Education Libraries*, 2002, Vol. 25(2), pp. 22–25	☐	☐

Referencing	True	False
When referencing two direct quotes from the same source and in sequence you can use ibid. to reference the second quote	☐	☐
The following are good examples of referencing in a bibliography:		
Tracy, E. 2002 *How to Study: a short introduction*. Sage	☐	☐
Buzan, T. (1995) *Use Your Head*. London, BBC Books	☐	☐
The following are good examples of referencing in an essay:		
as Johnson has noted, George Washington (1994) was an honest politician	☐	☐
'Washington always admitted when he had made a mistake' (Johnson, 1994: 117)	☐	☐

Writing skills

Essay writing	True	False
A word limit is only a vague guideline – you can exceed this by 30%	☐	☐
When writing essays you should use side margins of at least 1.5 cm to give the tutor space for comments	☐	☐
In an essay a line space is required for each new paragraph	☐	☐
An initial essay plan can be in the form of a diagram or chart	☐	☐
An essay plan is a rough draft of an essay	☐	☐
In an essay you should write down everything you know about the topic	☐	☐
In an essay question the term analyse means describing a topic in detail	☐	☐

Essay writing	True	False
In an essay every important point should be supported with reference to your reading	☐	☐
A good essay consists of accurately reproducing the ideas encountered in lectures and seminars	☐	☐
An essay shows that you have your own thoughts about the ideas encountered in lectures and seminars	☐	☐
The introduction must map out the content of the essay	☐	☐
The conclusion must refer back to the original question explored in the essay	☐	☐
The conclusion must reiterate the introduction almost exactly	☐	☐
A colloquial style is acceptable in an essay	☐	☐
You should always use the first person 'I' in an essay	☐	☐
A spellchecker will always spot all typographical errors	☐	☐
If you use a spellchecker then you don't need to proof-read your work	☐	☐

Analysis	True	False
'The impact of women's financial independence is less reliance on male breadwinners'. The key concept in this sentence is the term 'impact'	☐	☐
'High-level unemployment has a devastating effect on male workers'. The key concept in this sentence is the term 'effect'	☐	☐
'In the UK the expression "bogus asylum seeker" is used by politicians to discredit genuine refugees'. The key concept in this sentence is the term 'UK'	☐	☐
'The problem of poor housing is not just caused by lack of jobs'. The key concept in this sentence is the term 'poor'	☐	☐

Grammar	True	False
A noun is a name given to a person, place thing or idea	☐	☐
Common, proper, abstract and collective are types of noun	☐	☐
Personal, possessive, relative, interrogative and reflexive are all pronouns	☐	☐
Verbs are synonymous with adverbs	☐	☐
A conjunction is used to connect words or sentences	☐	☐
Verbs are about doing, being or having	☐	☐
An infinitive is acceptable as the sole verb in a sentence	☐	☐
Starting a sentence with 'but' is good practice	☐	☐
'Although' and 'however' can be used interchangeably	☐	☐
'Its' is an abbreviation of the expression 'it is'	☐	☐

Punctuation	True	False
A full stop is used to indicate the end of a sentence	☐	☐
Commas are always used after terms such as: however, finally, meanwhile	☐	☐
The use of the comma in this example is correct: 'standing on the bridge, he looked at the boats going down the river'	☐	☐
A comma or a semicolon can be used in lists	☐	☐
A colon is used to introduce a long direct quote	☐	☐
In an academic essay, exclamation marks are the best way to emphasise important points	☐	☐

Appendix G

Example of the feedback page 2004/5

Student: this feedback form was produced to test the scoring of the categories.

Student ID: xxxxxxx

* You scored 22 points in the ICT Skills section
* You scored 16 points in the Searching Skills section
* You scored 10 points in the Evaluation Skills section
* You scored 18 points in the Reference Skills section
* You scored 37 points in the Writing Skills section

The scoring system calculates two levels of competence: *advanced* or *novice* in the following areas covered by the Information Literacy module: ICT; Searching; Evaluating; Referencing; and Writing.

ICT
Advanced: 22–20
Novice: 19 or below

Searching
Advanced: 16
Novice: 15 or below

Evaluating
Advanced: 10
Novice: 9 or below

Referencing
Advanced: 18
Novice: 17 or below

Writing
Advanced: 37
Novice: 36 or below

General notes given to the students during the induction of the module:

- In order to complete the assessed portfolio for the information literacy module you will need to score at advanced level in all the categories of the skills covered by the questionnaire you have just completed.

- If you are a novice learner in any of these information literacy categories then it is necessary for you to practise these skills by completing the relevant tutorials (access to ilit.org and tutorials is demonstrated during the induction and this is complemented by step-by-step instructions that are included in the module booklet that students receive as part of the module information pack). The tutorials will address all the questions covered by the diagnostic questionnaire; therefore, by completing the exercises you will be able to complete the questionnaire and achieve advanced level in all the information literacy skills covered by this module.

Appendix H

Guidelines for the written application for funding

1. Purpose of grant

Grants are available for the conduct of primary research in Library and Information Sciences. The grant is £5,000 to fund projects starting from 1 January 2004 and ending on 1 December 2004.

2. Level and duration of awards

Applicants may bid for the sum of £5,000. Small Research Grants are tenable for the period covering 1 January 2004 to 1 December 2004. Assessors will evaluate the proposal on the basis of its academic merit, taking into account its originality; its relationship to, and the volume of, research already in the field; the scholarly importance of the research proposed; the feasibility of the research programme; the specificity of the scheme of research, presentation and intended outcomes.

3. Application and assessment procedures

Applications will be assessed by subject specialists through the evaluation of the following:

15-minute presentation of the application to a panel – this includes a Question and Answer session at the end of the presentation.

Submission of the final bid by: (date here)

4(a). Eligible costs

Grants may be sought to cover the direct expenses incurred in conducting the research, including:

- travelling costs
- consumables*
- specialist software
- staff development activities

* Consumables include the purchase of datasets, photocopies, microfilms, etc., and any other minor items that will be used up during the course of the project. Applicants may apply for short-term consultancy or salary costs for expert staff and for staff development activities required by the researcher to complete the project; costing to cover the organisation and running of workshops or seminars; attendance at conferences either in the UK or abroad.

4(b). Items not eligible for funding

Computer hardware (laptops, electronic notebooks, etc.), books and other permanent resources.

5. How to complete the form

Please complete in typescript throughout. Applicants may, if they wish, paste word-processed text on to the printed application form; or they may reproduce the entire form in a convenient word-processing package. *Applicants are requested to respect the regulations regarding font size and length of the individual sections.* Please use *10 point type size* for your answers to the questions.

Instructions for the application form individual sections

(Please provide a word count for sections specifying a word limit)

Personal details

Please note that all applications should include full details of the principal applicant.

Title of project

Please supply the title of the project. This should give a clear indication of the nature of the project proposed.

Financial details

Please state the sum requested to the nearest full pound. Applicants are advised to prepare careful costing for the proposed research expenses. Costs should be clearly itemised and justified in terms of the research programme. Please remember that grants are tenable for the period specified in point 3 above, and therefore costs must not extend beyond this period. It is essential that applicants clearly state the reasons why funds are needed. For example, it is not sufficient to state that the applicant will visit a particular archive: adequate details must be provided of sources to be consulted and the length of the visit must be clearly justified. Similarly, applicants are advised that travel costs should be fully itemised and, in case of prolonged absence, that the length of time for which subsistence is sought should be justified in the application.

Literature review

Applicants must include an appropriate literature review listing publications and research relevant to the field of enquiry explored by the proposal.

Scheme of research

Applicants are advised that adequate detail on the research proposal is required and this should be inserted in the space allocated. Please do not exceed 1,000 words. Ten point type size should be used (please do not reduce the type size below this). The proposal must:

- clearly specify the context and research objectives of the proposed study,
- describe the methodology to be used and provide a clear rationale for the sampling strategy adopted,
- set out a realistic research programme.

Output

Please identify the primary product of your research. In assessing value for money, the panel will take into account the intended outcome as compared with the amount of money sought, although it is fully appreciated that some modes of research are more expensive than others and proposals will not be discriminated against on the grounds of cost alone.

Plans for publication/dissemination

A great deal of importance is attached to the dissemination of research, and assessors will take into account how far the plans for publication or other dissemination strategies (e.g. workshop, website) have been developed.

Project schedule

A clear schedule for the project must be included identifying the estimated timetable of the research outcomes.

Personal statement

Applicants may supply a supporting personal statement to explain any unusual feature of their application, not accounted for elsewhere on the form.

Appendix I

Application for a Small Research Grant

Section a: Personal details

Applicant details

Surname Forename Employer's details

Address for correspondence

Postcode:
E-mail:

Section b: Title of project

Section c: Financial details

Grant requested (to the nearest full pound)

£

Particulars of costs

Give a breakdown of the total costs that will be incurred, specifying the particular items for which application is here being made to the Academy.

Item	Cost
Travel costs:	
Accommodation and daily maintenance (incorporating local travel costs) away from home: please state number of days and rate claimed, for each location	
Consumables: please state item and quantity required	
Research time: please state period of employment and hourly/monthly rate. Please specify how total period has been calculated (i.e. detailed breakdown of the costs)	
Other: please specify	
Total cost	£	Total sought	£

Section d: Literature review

Please provide a short review (500 words maximum) of the literature/ research projects that are relevant to the area of investigation proposed.

Section e: Scheme of research

Please provide a clear and comprehensive outline of the research project proposed (1,000 words maximum).

Section f: Output

Identify the primary product of your research (*please tick one or more as appropriate*).

(a) Evaluative report of an information-related service or policy	
(b) Creation of an electronic data resource	
(c) Creation of a new service in support of a specific user group	
(d) Other (please specify)	

Section g: Plans for publication/dissemination

Please describe the proposed output from the research, and outline your plans for publication or other dissemination of the research for which you are seeking an award. NB You should identify at least two dissemination strategies and provide a profile of the target audience.

Section h: Project schedule

Timetable	Details of activities

Section i: Personal statement

Applicants are invited to include any information relating to their professional career which they may wish to be taken into account in assessing this application (200 words maximum).

Appendix J

Information Literacy Questionnaire – AIR results[1]

1. What is your mode of study?

   Part-time   27
   Full-time   14

2. Are you:

   Male   7
   Female   34

3. Which age group do you belong to?

   18–19   0
   20–29   16
   30–39   16
   40–49   7
   50–59   2
   60+   0

4. Do you have access to the following?

	No	Yes
Computer at home	8	33
Internet at home	15	26

Information and Communication Technology (ICT) skills

5. Can you use the following facilities in the Windows environment?

	No	Yes
Open a window	0	41
Resize a window	3	38

	No	Yes
Minimise a window	0	40
Maximise a window	0	41
Manage folders	5	36
Copy files to folders	4	37
Copy files to disk	3	38
Format a disk	17	23
Back-up a disk	16	24
Print a word-processed document	1	39

6. On the Internet – can you complete the following tasks in the web browser Internet Explorer?

	No	Yes
Identify domain names	5	35
Create favourites	5	36
Edit favourites	10	30
Organise favourites in folders	16	24
Navigate through web pages	1	40
Use e-mail	1	40
Attach files to an e-mail	3	38
Use a search engine	1	40
Use a meta-search engine	13	27
Retrieve information from the invisible web	28	8

7. Presentation of printed information – can you word-process a document?

No	1
Yes	40

8. Can you produce a word-processed document with the following?

	No	Yes
Table of contents	5	36
Page numbers	2	39
Tables	10	31
Bullets	5	36
Graphics	15	23

	No	Yes
Charts	17	22
Spell-checked	1	40
Indents	8	31

Searching skills

9. Library skills – can you use the following library facilities?

	No	Yes
Author/title search	2	39
Keyword search	2	39
Date search	8	33
Borrower's information	2	39
Renew loans	4	37
Athens account	14	26
General references	7	34
Newspaper database	15	24

10. Search engine – can you apply the following searching strategies offered by the search engine of your choice?

	No	Yes
Keyword search	1	40
Phrase searching	3	38
Boolean operators	10	31
Field searching	14	26

Evaluation skills

11. Can you evaluate information in terms of the following criteria?

	No	Yes
Authority	14	26
Relevance	8	32
Accuracy	16	24
Currency	11	29
Scope	13	27

Note

1. In the original, the skip-path for people who have never used a computer is positioned after the personal details section. In the web version of this questionnaire this is activated when answering no to whether they have used a computer; the ICT and searching skills section are then skipped and the profile consists of the score for the evaluation section only. No student selected this option.

Appendix K
Homepage of ilit.org

The web pages that contain examples of tutorials supporting the information literacy practice explored in this book are accessed via the *Information Literacy DASS* option for the certificate-level module outlined in Chapter 5, and the *Applied Information Research* option for the postgraduate module, which is the focus of Chapter 6. See Figure A.1.

Most of the remaining options displayed on the ilit.org homepage do not have a direct bearing on the practice discussed here. However, the pages contain a variety of resources that information literacy educators may find relevant, and therefore a short summary is included here to aid their exploration:

- *Information Literacy Tutorials* – this option is structured using the SCONUL diagram,[1] which offers not only a map of the information literacy skills model but also provides access to tutorials fostering the development of these competences. The tutorials included here are produced either in house or are taken from other information literacy projects freely available on the Web.

- *Social Work IL* – this offers access to a dedicated web page that supports the development of basic information literacy within a social work certificate-level module. This provision was not included as a case study in this book because, unlike the information literacy provision for DASS and AIR, it does not subscribe to the embedded model of information literacy integration explored here.

- *Information Literacy Sources and Information Literacy Project* – these options are related to the ongoing research in information literacy I am undertaking at the Institute of Education, London, UK, and consist of the details of the literature and of projects reflecting the general debate on information literacy and its practice.

Figure A.1   The ilit.org homepage

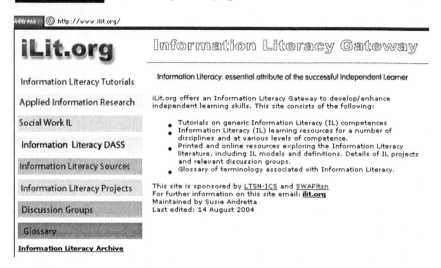

- *Information Literacy Archive* – this option is the newest addition to ilit.org and offers access to a web-based archive produced by the FURL software. Resources stored in this archive were collated during the writing of this book and therefore may be of some interest to information literacy educators.

- *Glossary* – this option provides a list of terms related to information literacy and that students are encouraged to consult as and when the need arises. This resource is taken from the Glossary of Internet & Web Jargon web page produced by UC Berkeley Library as part of its Teaching Library Internet Workshops: *http://www.lib.berkeley.edu/ TeachingLib/Guides/Internet/Glossary.html* (accessed 12 April 2004).

Note

1. The model is based on the original version predating the changes implemented by SCONUL in July 2004.

References

ACRL (Association of College and Research Libraries) (2000) *Information Literacy Competency Standards for Higher Education.* *http://www.ala.org/acrl/ilcomstan.html* (accessed 30 July 2004).

ALA (American Library Association) (1989) *ALA Presidential Committee on Information Literacy.* Washington, DC, 10 January 1989. *http://www.ala.org/ala/acrl/acrlpubs/whitepapers/presidential .htm* (accessed 7 March 2004).

ALA (American Library Association) (1998) *A Progress Report on Information Literacy. An Update on the ALA Presidential Committee on Information Literacy: Final Report.* *http://www.ala.org/ala/acrl/ acrlpubs/whitepapers/progressreport.htm* (accessed 7 March, 2004).

Albrecht, R. and Baron, S. (2002) 'Information literacy programmes: successes and challenges', *Journal of Library Administration*, 36 (1/2): 71–96.

Andretta, S. (2001) 'Legal information literacy: a pilot study', *New Library World*, 102 (1166/1167): 255–64.

Andretta, S. (2002) 'Information literacy for "mere mortals"', in P. Layzell Ward (ed.), *Continuing Professional Education for the Information Society.* Munich: K. G. Saur, pp. 105–14.

Andretta, S. (2003) 'Developing independent learning skills via the web', in U. O'Reilly (ed.), *4th Annual Conference of the LTSN Centre for Information and Computer Sciences*, 26–28 August 2003, Galway, pp. 251–2.

Andretta, S. (2004) 'Information literacy: developing the reflective information practitioner'. *Fifth Annual Conference of the LTSN Centre for Information and Computer Sciences*, 31 August – 2 September. Belfast (in press).

Andretta, S. and Cutting, A. (2003) 'Information literacy: a plug and play approach', *Libri*, 53 (3): 202–9.

Arp, L. (1990) 'Information literacy or bibliographic instruction: semantics or philosophy?', *RQ*, Fall: 46–9.

Bainton, T. (2001) 'Information Literacy and academic libraries: the SCONUL approach (UK/Ireland)'. *67th IFLA Council and General Conference Libraries and Librarians: Making a Difference in the Knowledge Age*, 16–21 August 2001, Boston: pp. 1–11.

Bawden, D. (2001) 'Information and digital literacies: a review of concepts', *Journal of Documentation*, 57 (2): 218–59.

Bawden, D. and Robinson, L. (2002) 'Promoting literacy in a digital age: approaches to training for information literacy', *Learned Publishing*, 15 (4): 297–301.

Big Blue Project, The (2001a) *http://www.leeds.ac.uk/bigblue/litreview .htm* (accessed 12 April 2004).

Big Blue Project, The (2001b) *http://www.leeds.ac.uk/bigblue/litreviewuk .html* (accessed 12 April 2004).

Booker, D. 'Introduction', in D. Booker (ed.), *Information Literacy: The Social Action Agenda*. Adelaide: University of South Australia Library, pp. i–iii.

Booth, A. and Fabian, C.A. (2002) 'Collaborating to advance curriculum based information literacy', *Journal of Library Administration*, 36 (1): 123–42.

Branch, C. and Gilchrist, D. (1996) 'Library literacy', *RQ*, 35 (4): 476–83.

Breivik, P.S. (1998) *Student Learning in the Information Age, American Council on Education, Series on Higher Education*. Phoenix, AZ: Oryx Press.

Bruce, C. (1997) *The Seven Faces of Information Literacy*. Adelaide: Auslib Press.

Bruce, C. (1999) 'Information Literacy. An international review of programs and research'. *Auckland '99 Lianza Conference*, 9–12 November 1999, pp. 1–9. *http://www2.auckland.ac.nz/lbr/conf99/ bruce.htm* (accessed 15 November 2001).

Bruce, C.S. (2002) 'Information Literacy as a Catalyst for Educational Change: A Background Paper', White Paper prepared for UNESCO, the US National Commission on Libraries and Information Science, and the National Forum on Information Literacy, for use at the *Information Literacy, Meetings of Experts*, Prague, The Czech Republic, July 2002, pp. 1–17. *http://www.nclis.gov/libinter/ infolitconf&meet/papers/bruce-fullpaper.pdf* (accessed 7 April 2004).

Bruce, C. and Candy, P. (eds) (2000) *Information Literacy Around the World*. Wagga Wagga: Australia Centre for Information Studies Charles Sturt University.

Bruss, N. and Macedo, D.P. (1985) 'Toward a pedagogy of the question: conversations with Paulo Friere', *Journal of Education*, 167: 7–21.

Bundy, A. (1996) 'Welcome: information literacy the key connection', in D. Booker (ed.), *Learning for Life. Information Literacy and the Autonomous Learner*. Adelaide: University of South Australia Library, pp. 1–2.

Bundy, A. (1999) *Information Literacy: the 21st Century Educational Smartcard*. Australian Academic & Research Libraries (AARL), pp. 233–50.

Bundy, A. (2000) 'Journey without end', in D. Booker (ed.), *Concept, Challenge, Conundrum: From Library Skills to Information Literacy*. Adelaide: University of South Australia Library, pp. 4–5.

Bundy, A. (2001) *Information Literacy: The Key Competency for the 21st Century. http://www.library.unisa.edu.au/papers/inlit21.htm* (accessed 8 November 2001).

Bundy, A. (2002) 'Information literacy: the bottom line', in D. Booker (ed.), *Information Literacy: The Social Action Agenda*. Adelaide: University of South Australia Library, pp. 1–2.

Bundy, A. (ed.) (2004) *Australian and New Zealand Information Literacy Framework principles, standards and practice*, 2nd edn. Adelaide: Australian and New Zealand Institute for Information Literacy.

Candy, P. (1996) 'Major themes and future directions', in Booker, D. (ed.), *Learning for Life: Information Literacy and the Autonomous Learner: Proceedings of the Second National Information Literacy Conference*. Adelaide: University of South Australia Library, p. 139.

Candy, P.C. (2002) 'Information Literacy and Lifelong Learning', White Paper prepared for UNESCO, the US National Commission on Libraries and Information Science, and the National Forum on Information Literacy, for use at the *Information Literacy, Meetings of Experts*, Prague: The Czech Republic, pp. 1–17. *http://www.nclis.gov/libinter/infolitconf&meet/papers/candy-paper.pdf* (accessed 7 April 2004).

Candy, P., Crebert, G. and O'Leary, J. (1994) *Developing Lifelong Learners Through Undergraduate Education*. Canberra: AGPS.

Carlson, R. and Repman, J. (2002) 'Building block of information literacy', *Education Libraries*, 25 (2): 22–5.

Carr, D. (1986) 'The meanings of the Adult Independent Library Learning Project', *Library Trends*, fall, 327–45.

CAUL (Council of Australian University Librarians) (2001) *Information Literacy Standards*, 1st edn. Canberra: CAUL.

CHE (Commission on Higher Education) (1994) *Characteristics of Excellence in Higher Education: Standards for Accreditation.* Middle States Association of Colleges and Schools.

CHE (Commission on Higher Education) (1995) 'Information Literacy Lifelong Learning in the Middle States Region'. *Boyer Commission on Educating Undergraduates in the Research University – Reinventing Undergraduate Education: a Blueprint for America's Research Universities,* pp. 1–19.

Cipolla, C. (1969) *Literacy and Development in the West.* Harmondsworth: Pelican; p69.

Creanor, L. and Durnell, H. (1994) 'Teaching information handling skills with hypertext', *Program,* 28 October: 349–65.

Curran, C. (1993) 'Information Literacy and the public librarian' in Kent, A. (ed) *Encyclopaedia of Library and Information Science* vol. 51: pp. 257–66. New York: Marcel Dekker.

De Ruiter, J. (2002) 'Aspects of dealing with digital information: 'mature' novices on the internet, *Library Trends,* Fall, 199–209.

Dillon, C., Needham, G., Hodgkinson L., Parker J. and Baker K. (2003) 'Information literacy at The Open University a developmental approach', in A. Martin and H. Rader (eds) *Information and IT Literacy Enabling Learning in the 21st Century.* London: Facet Publishing, pp. 66–76.

Doherty, J.J., Hansen, M.A. and Kaya, K.K. (1999) 'Teaching information skills in the information age: the need for critical thinking', *Library Philosophy and Practice,* 1 (2): 1–12. *http://www.webpages.uidaho.edu/~mbolin/doherty.htm* (accessed 22 April 2004).

Doyle, C. (1992) 'Outcome measures for information literacy within the National Education Goals of 1990'. *Final report to National Forum on Information Literacy. Summary of Findings.* National Forum for Information Literacy ED351033.

Drew, S. (1998) *Key Skills in Higher Education: Background and Rationale.* Staff and Educational Development Association Special No. 6.

Ennis, K. (2001) 'Information skills – the final frontier', *The Library Association Record,* 103 (5): 292–3.

Executive Advisory Group to CILIP (2002) *CILIP in the Knowledge Economy: A Leadership Strategy.* London: Chartered Institute of Library and Information Professionals.

Friere, B. (1974) *Pedagogy of the Oppressed.* Penguin.

Ford, B. (1995) 'Information literacy as a barrier', *IFLA Journal,* 21 (2): 99–101.

Goodwin, P. (2003) 'Information literacy, but at what level?', in A. Martin and H. Rader (eds), *Information and IT Literacy Enabling Learning in the 21st Century*. London: Facet Publishing, pp. 88–97.

Grafstein, A. (2002) 'A discipline-based approach to information literacy', *Journal of Academic Librarianship*, 197–204.

Hara, K. (1997) 'The effects of resource-based instruction on the acquisition of information skills', *Education Libraries Journal*, 40 (1): 17–24.

Hepworth, M. (1999) 'A study of undergraduate information literacy and skills: the inclusion of information literacy and skills in the undergraduate curriculum'. *65th IFLA Council and General Conference*. Bangkok. *htpp://www.ifla.org/IV/ifla65/papers/107-124e.htm* (accessed 8 November 2001).

Hepworth, M. (2000) 'Approaches to providing information literacy training in higher education: challenges for librarians', *The New Review of Academic Librarianship*, 21–34.

Illich, I.D. (1976) *Deschooling Society*. Pelican Books.

Johnson, II. (2003) The SCONUL Task Force on Information Skills, in A. Martin and H. Rader (eds), *Information and IT Literacy Enabling Learning in the 21st Century*. London: Facet Publishing, pp. 45–52.

Kendall, M. and Booth, H. (2003) 'Developing generic online tutorials as a strategy for extending the use of WebCT. *4th Annual Conference of the LTSN Centre for Information and Computer Sciences*, 26–28 August, Galway, pp. 21–6.

King, A. (1993) 'From sage on the stage to guide on the side', *College Teaching*, 41 (1): 30–5.

Kirk, T.G. (2002) *Information Literacy in a Nutshell: Basic Information for Academic Administrators and Faculty*, Institute for Information Literacy (IIL). *http:www.ala.org/acrl/nili/whatis.html* (accessed 12 December 2002).

Knight, L.A. (2002) 'The role of assessment in library user education', *Reference Services Review*, 30 (1): 15–24.

Kuhlthau, C.C. (1988) 'Winter, developing a model of the library search process: cognitive and affective aspects', *RQ*, 232–42.

Lawson, M.D. (1999) 'Assessment of a college freshman course in information resources', *Library Review*, 48 (2): 73–8.

Lenox, M.F. and Walker, M.L. (1992) 'Information literacy: challenge for the future', *International Journal of Information and Library Research*, 4: 1–18.

Lichtenstein, A.A. (2000) 'Informed instruction: learning theory and information literacy', *Journal of Educational Media & Library Sciences*, 38 (1): 22–31.

Long, K. (1989) *American Forecaster Almanac 1990*. Philadelphia: Running Press Book Publishers.

Lupton, M. (2004) *The Learning Connection. Information Literacy and the Student Experience*. Adelaide: Auslib Press.

MacDonald, R. (2002) *Plagiarism Prevention, Detection and Punishment*. Briefing paper 6 version 1, Issued October 2002. *http://dbweb.liv.ac.uk/ltsnpsc/briefing_papers/plag6.htm* (accessed 10 April 2004).

Martin, A. (2003) 'Towards e-literacy', in A. Martin and H. Rader (eds), *Information and IT Literacy*. London: Facet Publishing, pp. 3–23.

Mayer, E., 1996. 'Opening address: Information literacy and the autonomous learner', in Booker, D. (ed.), *Learning for Life. Information Literacy and the Autonomous Learner*, Adelaide: University of South Australia Library, pp. 3–5.

McFarlan, D.D. and Chandler, S. (2002) '"Plug and play" in context: reflections on a distance information literacy unit', *Journal of Business and Finance Librarianship*, 7 (2/3): 115–30.

McInnis, R. and Symes, D.S. (1991) 'Running backwards from the finish line: a new concept for bibliographic instruction', *Library Trends*, 39 (3): 223–37.

Mellon, C.A., 1988. 'Information problem-solving: a developmental approach to library instruction', in C. Oberman and K. Strauch (eds), *Theories of Bibliographic Education*. New Providence, NJ: R.R. Bowker LLC, pp. 75–89.

Moore, P. (2002) 'An Analysis of Information Literacy Education' Worldwide White paper prepared for UNESCO, the US National Commission on Libraries and Information Science, and the National Forum on Information Literacy, for the use at the *Information Literacy Meeting of Experts*, Prague, The Czech Republic, July, pp. 1–17. *http://www.nclis.gov/libinter/infolitconf&meet/papers/moore-fullpaper.pdf* (accessed 7 April 2004).

Mutch, A. (1997) 'Information literacy: an exploration', *International Journal of Information Management*, 17 (5): 377–86.

Oberman, C. (1991) 'Avoiding the cereal syndrome, or critical thinking in the electronic environment', *Library Trends*, 39 (3): 189–202.

Oberman, C. and Linton, R.A. (1988) 'Guided design: teaching library research as problem-solving' in C. Oberman, C. and K. Strauch (eds), *Theories of Bibliographic Education*. New Providence, NJ: R.R. Bowker LLC, pp. 111–34.

O'Brien, R. (1998) *An Overview of the Methodological Approach of Action Research*. *http://www.web.net/~robrien/papers/arfinal.html* (accessed 5 March 2004).

OECD (2002) *Knowledge and Skills for Life: First Results From PISA 2000*. *http://www.pisa.oecd.org/knowledge/home/intro.htm*.

Orr, D., Appleton, M. and Wallin, M. (2001) 'Information literacy and flexible delivery: creating a conceptual framework and model', *Journal of Academic Librarianship*, 457–63.

O'Sullivan, C. (2002) 'Is Information literacy relevant in the real world?' *New Library World*, 30 (1): 7–14.

Owusu-Ansah, E.K. (2004) 'Information literacy and higher education: placing the academic library in the center of a comprehensive solution', *Journal of Academic Librarianship*, 3–16.

Paul, R. (1992) 'Critical thinking: what, why and how', *New Directions for Community Colleges*, 77 (18-2): 3–24.

Peacock, J. (2004) 'Standards, curriculum and learning: implications for professional development', in A. Bundy (ed.), *Australian and New Zealand Information Literacy Framework principles, standards and practice*, 2nd edn. Adelaide: Australian and New Zealand Institute for Information Literacy, pp. 29–33.

Rader, H.B. (1991) 'Information literacy: a revolution in the library', *RQ*, fall, 25–9.

Rader, H.B. (2002a) 'Information Literacy – An emerging Global Priority', White Paper prepared for UNESCO, the US National Commission on Libraries and Information Science, and the National Forum on Information Literacy, for the use at the *Information Literacy Meeting of Experts*, Prague, The Czech Republic, July. *http://www.nclis.gov/libinter/infolitconf&meet/rader-fullpaper.html* (accessed 20 April 2004).

Rader, H.B. (2002b) 'Information literacy 1973–2002: a selected review', *Library Trends*, 51 (fall): 242–59.

Rader, H.B. (2003) 'Information literacy – a global perspective', in A. Martin and H. B. Rader (eds), *Information and IT Literacy*. London: Facet Publishing, pp. 24–42.

Ray, K. and Day, J. (1998) 'Students attitudes towards electronic resources', *Information Research*. *http://www.shef.ac.uk/is/publications/infres/paper54.html* (accessed 16 November 2001).

Repman, J. and Carlson, R. (2002) 'Building blocks for information literacy', *Education Libraries* 25 (winter): 22–5.

Robson, C. (2002) *Real World Research*, 2nd edn. Oxford: Blackwell.

Rockman, I.F. (2002) 'Strengthening connections between information literacy, general education and assessment efforts', *Library Trends*, fall, 185–97.

Schön, D. (1991) *The Reflective Practitioner. How Professionals Think in Action*. UK: Ashgate Publishing Ltd.

SCONUL (1999) *Information Skills in Higher Education*: a SCONUL position paper. Prepared by the Information Skills Task Force, on behalf of SCONUL.

Shapiro, J.J. and Hughes, K. (1996) 'Information Literacy as a Liberal Art. Enlightenment proposal for a new curriculum', March/April. *http://www.educause.edu/pub/er/review/reviewarticles/31231.html* (accessed 16 February 2004).

Sherrat, C.S. and Schlabach, M.L. (1990) 'The application of concept mapping in reference and information services', *RQ*, fall: 60–9.

Smart, J. (2003) 'Review of "Information and IT literacy: Enabling Learning in the 21st Century"', *Freepint*, No. 149. *http://www.freepint.com/issues/201103.htm* (accessed 11 December 2003).

Snavely, L. (2001) 'Information literacy standards for higher education: an international perspective'. *67th IFLA Council and General Conference*, 16–21 August, pp. 1–4.

Snavely, L. and Cooper, N. (1997) 'The information literacy debate', *Journal of Academic Librarianship*, 23 January: 9–14.

Stern, C. (2003) 'Measuring students' information literacy competency', in A. Martin and H. Rader (eds), *Information and IT Literacy Enabling Learning in the 21st Century*. London: Facet Publishing, pp. 112–9.

Town, J.S. (2003) 'Information literacy and the information society', in S. Hornby and Z. Clarke (eds), *Challenge and Change in the Information Society*. London: Facet Publishing, pp. 81–103.

Virkus, S. (2003) 'Information literacy in Europe: a literature review', *Information Research*, 8 July. *http://informationr.net/ir/8-4/paper159.html* (accessed 7 April 2004).

Webber, S. (2003) 'Review of the IT and Information Literacy Conference', *March*, 2002: 'Getting the knowledge'. *http://dis.shef.ac.uk/literacy/itilreview.htm* (accessed 12/07/2004).

Webber, S. and Johnston, B. (2000) 'Conceptions of information literacy: new perspectives and implications', *Journal of Information Science*, 26 (6): 381–97.

Webber, S. and Johnston, B. (2003) 'Assessment for information literacy: vision and reality', in A. Martin and H. Rader (eds), *Information and IT Literacy*. London: Facet Publishing, pp. 101–1.

Index

IL is an abbreviation for 'Information Literacy', and HE for 'Higher Education'

ANZIIL, 43–4, 153–9
SCONUL, 44–6, 161–2
see also the entries for each organisation
functional literacy, 19, 33

generic information skills, 9, 44
Griffiths University, 52
guide on the side, 60–2, 121

higher/lower order thinking/learning, 13–14, 41, 46–8
House of Representatives Committee for Long-Term Strategies, 29

ICT skills/strategies, 26, 32, 34, 45–6, 172–3 – *see also* case studies
ilit.org – *see* case study 2: website
illiteracy – *see* literacy
independent learning, 23, 96, 98, 106, 107, 118, 137–8
– *see also* learning how to learn
information anxiety, 8
information awareness, 45–6, 65, 84, 119
information ethics, 41–3, 84
information explosion, 8, 24
Information Industry Association, 26
information literacy:
  competencies, 27, 43, 46, 47–8, 64, 84, 96, 98, 102, 121
  curriculum, 11, 59
  and education, 7, 15–16, 27, 59
  educators, 1, 52, 55, 58, 65, 136, 137, 138, 193–4
  embedded, 15, 19, 22, 49, 56, 102, 106, 107, 113
  good practice, 51, 52
  institution-wide, 50, 51–4
  interest in, 12, 36

IQ (Institutional Quotient) test, 52, 167–70
multifaceted, 12–14, 16
as a pedagogical tool, 13, 53–4, 139, 140
principles, 28–9, 60, 79–80
programme components, 59, 69–74
responsibility for, 32, 37, 52, 53
skills, 8–9, 50, 51, 65, 67, 68, 80, 82, 84, 86, 88–90, 92–6, 100–1
stages, 15, 18, 47, 113
use of term, 19–20
Information Literacy Competency Standards for HE – *see* ACRL
Information Literacy: the Australian Agenda (Conference), 30
Information Literacy: the Professional Issue (Conference), 31
Information Literacy: the Social Action Agenda (Conference), 31
information management, 16, 25, 110
information overload, 9, 24, 25, 92, 98
information professionals and IL, 27, 31–2, 34–5 – *see also* case study 2
information retention, 11, 65
Information Skills in HE (SCONUL), 34, 161–2
information society, 5, 19, 24–5, 28, 29
information superhighway, 24
inquiry-based learning, 27
Institute of Information Literacy, 27
Institution-wide collaboration
  – *see* collaboration
institutional context of IL, 139–40
institutional hostility, 139
integration of IL, 26, 27, 34–5, 49–50, 55–6, 109, 135
  multilevel, 50–1
  subject, 43, 58–9, 105–6

DATE DUE

GAYLORD

PRINTED IN U.S.A.